"Dan DeWitt's book packs a wallop. The conversational style masks a deep acquaintance with the major issues and philosophies of the day. DeWitt successfully shows how behind every apparently rational objection to faith lies a moral and 'religious' commitment, which can be shaken only by a gospel jolt. Winsome and engaging, this text is must reading for any aspiring Christian apologist."

William Edgar, Professor of Apologetics, Westminster Theological Seminary

"I'm kind of over apologetics-type books. Many—if not most—portray conversations with skeptics in this weird alternate reality where unbelievers ask all the right questions in the right order and care about intellectual consistency. Dan DeWitt knows that world doesn't exist. And in *Christ or Chaos* he shows how fluid and complex journeys to and from Christ really are. Still, he avoids wandering through spiritual-sounding truisms. DeWitt is not afraid of arguments and facts. Like all his writing, this book anthologizes some of the most compelling reflections from Christianity's best thinkers. *Christ or Chaos* wrestles with the deepest questions without the familiar cookie cutters."

Aaron Cline Hanbury, Editorial Director, *Relevant* magazine

"*Christ or Chaos* gets right to the heart of the biggest human question: Are we made by God with a plan, or are we a cosmic accident? With stories, research, and personal examples, Dan will take you on a journey exploring the most important questions of life. And as you will see, the evidence for the Christian worldview is compelling."

Sean McDowell, Assistant Professor of Christian Apologetics, Biola University; author, *A New Kind of Apologist*

"Change begins with conversations. With compassion-filled logical prose, DeWitt's *Christ or Chaos* provides believers with an accessible icebreaker so that they can begin thoughtful long-term conversations with the nonbelieving world."

D. A. Horton, Pastor, The Summit Church, Durham, North Carolina; author, *Bound to Be Free*

"In *Christ or Chaos* DeWitt uses argument in an artistic way to illustrate the biblical view of the world. He shows not only that Christianity is true, but also that it is the only compelling way to understand the cosmos and the human condition. This is a great read."

FLAME, Grammy-nominated Christian hip-hop artist

"In this book Dan applies eternal truth to modern ideologies in a way that engages and equips every reader to discover or defend his or her faith. All who care about spiritual truth owe it to themselves to read this book."

Russ Lee, award-winning singer/songwriter; lead singer, NewSong

"DeWitt weighs the evidence for and against Christianity theologically, cleverly, and profoundly, yet with sensitivity and clarity. In the end, he reminds us that only the gospel can change the human heart and enlighten the mind. If you want to be prepared to answer difficult questions about the reality of your Christian faith in the public arena in a gentle and reverent way, this book is for you. I thoroughly enjoyed reading it and I will recommend it frequently."

Miguel Núñez, Senior Pastor, International Baptist Church,
Santo Domingo, Dominican Republic; President, Wisdom and Integrity

CHRIST
OR
CHAOS

Dan DeWitt

Foreword by Josh Wilson

WHEATON, ILLINOIS

Cover design: Jeff Miller, Faceout Studio

Cover image: Neo Edmund/Shuttertock

First printing 2016

Printed in the United States of America

Scripture quotations are from the ESV® Bible (The Holy Bible, English Standard Version®), copyright © 2001 by Crossway, a publishing ministry of Good News Publishers. Used by permission. All rights reserved.

Trade paperback ISBN: 978-1-4335-4896-3
ePub ISBN: 978-1-4335-4899-4
PDF ISBN: 978-1-4335-4897-0
Mobipocket ISBN: 978-1-4335-4898-7

Library of Congress Cataloging-in-Publication Data
DeWitt, Dan, 1977–
Christ or chaos / Dan DeWitt; foreword by Josh Wilson.
   pages cm
   Includes bibliographical references and index.
   ISBN 978-1-4335-4896-3 (tp)
   1. Christianity and atheism. 2. Apologetics. I. Title.
BR128.A8D485   2016
261.2'1—dc23   2015019152

Crossway is a publishing ministry of Good News Publishers.

VP		26	25	24	23	22	21	20	19	18	17	16
15	14	13	12	11	10	9	8	7	6	5	4	3	2	1

To my big brother, Chris,
with much love and respect

Contents

Foreword

You know the feeling you get when you're relaxing in a chair, leaning back, arms up, fingers folded behind your head, and all of a sudden you recline just a little too far? Right after you suck all the air out of the room, one of two things happens. The first is that by flailing your arms in just the right direction at just the right speed, you somehow manage to right yourself and find your balance. The alternative is that you fall flat on your back, wind knocked out, probably needing to take a few moments to recover from your not-so-graceful plunge.

That second outcome: that's me when I went to college. My dad is a pastor, I was raised in the church, and I grew up with mostly Christian friends. I was taught that what I believed was the absolute truth, no ifs, ands, or buts about it. All the way through my high school career, I can't remember doubting much about my faith. I was comfortable, leaning back in my cushy Christian recliner, confident that I had this faith thing figured out.

Then, in college, I met people who believed differently than me. Some of them followed other religions. Others were atheists or agnostics. But one thing we all had in common was that we were basically decent people, adhering to a fairly similar set of moral guidelines. I didn't really know any atheists in high school, and out of my naiveté, I assumed they were probably all immoral or uncaring, and obviously not very thoughtful since they didn't believe in God. What I found was quite the opposite. These folks became my friends. As I got to know them, I realized that they were intelligent and incredibly thoughtful. They just happened to subscribe to a completely different worldview.

My chair collapsed and I spiraled, arms thrashing, into the abyss of confusion. I began to wonder if my faith was ill placed. I wasn't sure if there were good, rational reasons to believe in Christianity. I considered, for the first time, that some other religion might have it right or, even scarier, that there might be no God at all.

About that time, I met someone named Dan DeWitt, who became my college pastor at church. Dan was exactly who I needed to have in my life during those frightening moments of rebuilding my faith. Dan had been down the path I was on, and knew well how to respond to my doubts. He listened with grace, prayed with and for me, and helped me sort through *why* I believe *what* I believe. He took his time and didn't give me a one-size-fits-all solution.

Dan wasn't afraid of my doubts, I learned, because God isn't afraid of our doubts. I came to see my growing list of questions not as a sign of a weak faith, but as an indicator that I was taking my faith seriously. I learned to view my doubts as opportunities, as an invitation to search for truth.

One of the things I appreciate about Dan is that he is a Christian leader who's not afraid to publicly empathize with skeptics. He won't tell you he has it all figured out, because none of us do. But he will consistently point you toward the great Love and Light that has captured his heart.

Jesus is big enough to handle your uncertainty. He isn't intimidated by your questions. That's because he's not a formula, but a real person. And in the end, what will change your life is not an argument, but the very Spirit of God. And I'm praying that's exactly what will happen as you work through the following pages.

This book is Dan's way of catching your recliner. It's his way of pulling up a chair alongside of yours for a friendly dialogue about the most serious of topics: truth that *can* be defended, but doesn't need defending; the love of God that isn't deserved, but is given freely; and a peculiar providence that places people, and even books like this one, in our lives at just the right time. Maybe you'll discover, perhaps even for the first time, a faith strong enough to support you with all of your questions and doubts.

Josh Wilson
singer/songwriter

Introduction

Reality Used to Be
a Friend of Mine

Thirst was made for water; inquiry for truth.
C. S. Lewis, *The Great Divorce*

The sun will probably kill us.

That's what scientists tell us. The large warmth-giving star our earth orbits around will continue to heat up until it burns all its nuclear fuel. Feeding its insatiable hunger for energy, it will grow into what experts call a "Red Giant." In its hot wrath this giant will gobble up all life on earth and burp out a silent planet.

The End.

That's how the curtain closes in one storyline at least. And that's the outlook many embrace today. The plot begins in a murky prebiotic ocean and ends in the heat death of all of civilization. And if that's where life came from and where history is headed, there's not much we can do about it. After all, wishful thinking has never slain a giant.

I loved giant stories as a kid. They involved mysterious beans, cunning heroes, and defeated Goliaths. But the Red Giant isn't my idea of an inspirational fairy tale. I think I like the Jolly Green Giant, who advertises canned vegetables on television, a whole lot better.

If it were up to me, the Green Giant would trounce the Red Giant, and we would all walk off into the sunset holding hands and snacking on sweet peas. In all seriousness, there actually is a fifty-five-foot-tall statue of the Jolly Green Giant in Blue Earth, Minnesota. If things end the way scientists predict, this monument will one day melt beneath the heat of the expanding sun, a reminder that life doesn't have to mirror fantasy.

Not every story has a happy ending. Not all giants are jolly. When I was a child I thought like a child. Perhaps it's time to put away childish things.

But we're all suckers for a good story. That's why we squirm a bit at gloomy projections for the human race. We want a comedy even though our meteorological forecast forces us into a tragedy. I think deep down we're all holding out hope for a David figure to step in with a humble sling and defend us from the cosmic foe threatening our existence. We simply want a better ending.

Choose Your Own Adventure

Every perspective of reality contains an inherent narrative. Every worldview is a novel. Each has an author, a beginning, and an end. The task for thinking people is to consider not which story is the most interesting, but which one is actually true. In the end we may find a story compelling and true in which we can lose ourselves. Better yet, we may discover a story in which we can actually *find* ourselves. That would be novel indeed.

As a young boy I enjoyed reading the Choose Your Own Adventure books. At the end of each short chapter you would be asked a question about the plot and then be directed to a specific page to continue the story, depending on your answer. While every decision along the way would influence the outcome, none was more important than the very first. Your response to the first question would determine the scope of all of your future options.

Reality works a lot like this. We all have to make fundamental assumptions about the nature of the universe. The first chapter of the human narrative presents the question about origins. The options are (a) nature contains the answer to this question or (b) something outside nature contains the answers. The decisions that follow are important, but this first choice determines the possibilities—the parameters—of the rest of the plot.

This is the basic worldview assumption that Thomas is forced to wrestle with his junior year in college. His roommate, Zach, has recently become an atheist. Zach is convinced that his new worldview offers a superior explanation of the universe. Encouraging Thomas to reconsider his faith, Zach has suggested that Christianity is irrational and detached from reality.

The two have been best friends since they were little kids. Very few of their childhood memories do not include the other in some way. Rooming together in college was a given. They've looked forward to it since their senior year in high school when they decided to attend the same university. But now, in their third year of college life, it seems they've never been further apart.

This has both taxed their friendship and challenged Thomas's faith. He fears it may drive them apart forever. How can their friendship survive such a clash?

To be honest, many a night Thomas has wondered if his roommate is right. On occasion he has asked himself, "Is Christianity really disconnected from the world? Is religious belief irrational?"

What most troubles him is that some of Zach's arguments against Christianity seem reasonable and persuasive. After all, they've both seen some really unfortunate things in the church. Thomas doesn't have to be convinced of the limitations of their religious upbringing or of the evils done in the name of faith. So in many ways he empathizes with Zach's decision to walk away.

And he's considered what it would mean to follow in his footsteps.

On the other hand, if atheism is true, then the grand story of humanity means basically that we are the products of time and chance and are headed toward nonexistence. We are simply matter in motion—entropy in sneakers. But to Thomas the human experience seems to point the opposite direction. Is this only wishful thinking?

Thomas has always considered the biblical description of the world to line up with his lived experience. For him, Christianity has always made sense of life. So he's not ready to give up without a fight. Yet his roommate has raised some valid questions about belief in God. Given the topic and their lifelong friendship, this is no trivial debate he can brush off.

Thankfully, this isn't a journey Thomas has to take alone. He finds support from a campus ministry leader who offers some helpful resources for responding to Zach's challenge. They talk late one evening and develop a list of biblical themes we should expect to encounter in the real world if Christianity is indeed true.

Thomas's list includes things like a universe that is not eternal, telltale signs of design in creation, a universal longing for God (or a God substitute), a moral fabric to the universe, and accounts of God interacting in history. If Christianity is true, we should expect to find these things in the world around us and in the human experience.

If Christianity is irrational, then it should be easy enough to expose this and demonstrate that its explanation of the world and human lives is incoherent and uncompelling. But if Christianity is true, then it should provide insights into the world we live in, the values we hold, and the lives we seek to lead.

Is reality best explained by cosmos or chaos? The word *cosmos* is used to refer to the universe as an orderly system. The word *chaos* refers to something governed by chance. Which word best describes our world? Do we live in a cosmos or a chaos? Does Christianity lead us to understand the cosmos in a way that makes sense of our lived experience? Christianity, if true, should offer a map to reality—a guide to understanding the cosmos.

The Next Steps

In these pages we will follow Thomas as he reevaluates his faith in light of his roommate's challenge that Christianity is irrational. I hope to provide an honest portrayal of what faith and friendship look like when they're held in tension. And I hope to demonstrate the gospel's relevance in the contemporary landscape of skepticism.

Like my earlier book *Jesus or Nothing*, I use a narrative framework with fictional characters to illustrate what it might look like to work through issues in real-life situations. Each chapter focuses on a different aspect of Christianity that Thomas considers important and how it relates to his experience. I interweave some of the arguments for and against the Christian worldview in an attempt to depict what these kinds of dialogues can look and sound like. I recognize that my bias as a Christian will affect the way I present either side.

I take this approach because I happen to think the gospel is up to the challenge. I'm concerned that many Christians are content to hunker down in Christian echo chambers and ignore the broader cultural conversations about faith in God. Some treat the gospel like a fragile heirloom that should be covered in Bubble Wrap, hidden in the attic, and thus preserved for future generations.

I tend to think the gospel can hold its own. The gospel won't be intimidated or overshadowed by rival truth claims. As the famous preacher Charles Spurgeon said, you don't defend a lion. Unchain it and it will defend itself.

This book is about the gospel minus the Bubble Wrap. It's about the gospel's power unshackled and taken out of the attic. We need the gospel more than it needs us. And we see the gospel best when we actually see through it—when it's like a pair of reading glasses giving us a clear vision of reality.

That's why Christians should never be ashamed of the gospel in the private or public domain, in our churches or in the marketplace of ideas. We shouldn't shiver at the thought of subjecting the gospel to the test of sincere scrutiny. If it's false, then we have nothing to gain, and if it's true, we have nothing to lose. As C. S. Lewis once said, "One must keep on pointing out that Christianity is a statement which, if false, is of no importance, and, if true, of infinite importance. The one thing it cannot be is moderately important."[1]

This may be a good place to offer a disclaimer: I make frequent references to Lewis throughout this book. I teach a class on Lewis a couple times every year at Boyce College, and in all my reading related to worldview analysis I find that few writers illustrate worldview thinking in terms of their private lives, public debates, and published works as well as he does.

I've written this book for students like Thomas who are torn between faith and friendship. I've also written this book for students like Zach who have walked away from the gospel. My prayer is that somewhere between their polar positions, through the ambient noise of skeptics and religious sound bites, a healthy conversation can take place about what Christianity looks like in the real world—or better yet—what the real world looks like in Christianity.

1

Much Ado about Nothing

> For what you see and hear depends a good
> deal on where you are standing: it also de-
> pends on what sort of person you are.
>
> C. S. Lewis, *The Magician's Nephew*

The twentieth-century journalist and Christian apologist G. K. Chesterton once said, "There are two ways of getting home; and one of them is to stay there. The other is to walk round the whole world till we come back to the same place."[1] Chesterton's point was that truth might be closer than you realize, perhaps right under your nose. And sometimes, like with the prodigal son, truth is found at the end of a long road back to the Father's house.

Chesterton was specifically speaking of Christianity. And in his book *The Everlasting Man* he contrasted two helpful forms of analyzing the Christian faith. The first is from the inside. The second is from a million miles away. As he said, "The best relation to our spiritual home is to be near enough to love it. But the next best is to be far enough away not to hate it."[2]

In other words, sometimes stepping just outside the front door of a particular worldview leaves you too close to have a clear perspective. You can be standing beneath the awning while complaining of the shade. Your proximity itself creates emotional and intellectual blind spots.

As Chesterton put it, "The popular critics of Christianity are not really outside of it. . . . Their criticism has taken on a curious tone; as of a random and illiterate heckling."[3] The modern-day terrain of heckling, as Chesterton describes it, is fraught with emotional landmines and intellectual blockades. Safe passage to meaningful conversations can be hard to find.

A Bridge over Troubled Waters

The well-known literary critic C. S. Lewis navigated this terrain as a young man. Lewis describes this journey in his first published work after his conversion to Christianity, *The Pilgrim's Regress*. A fictional account of his conversion, the book was written over a holiday visit with his childhood best friend. Lewis patterned the work after John Bunyan's classic *The Pilgrim's Progress*.

Like Bunyan, Lewis used allegory to make his point. But his "regress" offers a glaring contrast to Bunyan's "progress." Lewis wanted to illustrate that his character found spiritual fulfillment not by progressing to a far-off land to be freed from a heavy burden, but in the fulfillment of a longing that, as he learned, could take place only in the Christianity he had rejected from his youth. He found progress by turning around and retracing his steps.

Sometimes that's what progress looks like: turning around and heading back the other way. It can hardly be called progress if we are simply going further down the road but heading the wrong direction.

Lewis later described this in his autobiographical work *Surprised by Joy*: "But then the key to my books is Donne's maxim, 'The heresies that men leave are hated most.' The things I assert most vigorously are those that I resisted long and accepted late."[4]

As a young man Lewis walked away from his spiritual upbringing. And it took some time for him to get far enough away to no longer hate it. But then he came back close enough to learn to love it. He walked around an entire world just to come back home.

I've seen this process myself. I've known some who have walked away from Christianity and now find it difficult, whether they acknowledge it or not, to engage in a careful and considerate conversation about the faith. As Donne said, they hate most the heresies they have personally left. They've walked away from Christianity. And now they despise it.

You've probably known someone who fits that description. They dismiss Christianity with visceral hatred, yet go on to talk about the virtues of Muslim prayers, or the value of Buddhist meditation, or the solitude of Hindu temples. They are, according to Chesterton, still too close to see clearly. That's because proximity matters.

I've experienced what may be akin to a skeptic's rejection of Christianity, though my story doesn't involve losing faith in God. In the middle of my college years I made a decisive break with the brand of Baptist fundamentalism I had grown up with. I didn't renounce faith in God or anything like that, but I did leave the denomination of my childhood.

It took me a few years to get over it, to be honest. I was bitter—probably because I was hurt. It was hard to even talk about it without feelings of resentment welling to the surface. I channeled my anger through public expression in a way that I now find unfortunate. Not necessarily because I have come around to change my opinion per se, but rather because I realize that emotional tirades aren't synonymous with compelling arguments.

I think about this when I read the e-mails or Facebook posts of friends who have left Christianity and embraced atheism. Though I don't assume I understand their journey, I think I can empathize a little, as can many who may be more objective than I was in the face of similar emotional unrest.

This tendency is illustrated in a 2013 article by Larry Taunton, "Listening to Young Atheists: Lessons for a Stronger Christianity," published in *The Atlantic*. After traveling

to numerous college campuses and surveying students in various skeptic organizations, Taunton made six summary observations: (1) these students all had religious backgrounds of some kind; (2) they felt the mission and message of their childhood churches were vague; (3) they felt their churches offered superficial answers to their serious questions; (4) they had respect for leaders who took their questions seriously; (5) the ages between fourteen and seventeen were crucial in their later decision to become atheists; (6) and their decision to leave the faith was discussed primarily in emotional categories.[5]

Taunton's observations offer insight on the traction that the new atheist movement has gained since 9/11 and the subsequent publication of Sam Harris's book *The End of Faith*. The new atheist authors have a receptive audience with young people who have left the church. And the emotional nature of their decisions, as described by Taunton, can make it difficult to build bridges for meaningful conversations.

Dueling Evangelists

Thomas has tended to ignore the banter of public atheists like Richard Dawkins. So much of the exchange between Christians and atheists in mainstream media is unfortunately filled with anger and scorn. But Thomas can't ignore his roommate, Zach. They're lifelong friends. They're in it for the long haul, as the saying goes.

But when Zach comes out as an atheist, Thomas is at a

loss for how to respond. The resentment Zach now feels toward his religious past can make things awkward between them at times. Thomas represents something he wants to leave behind. But Zach doesn't want to leave Thomas behind. It's complicated.

Thomas is also committed to their friendship, and deep down he hopes one day Zach will find his way back. But Zach is hoping Thomas will come to see things his way. So, it's a bit of an evangelistic arm-wrestling match.

Some Christians might be surprised by the amount of resources designed to help skeptics deconvert Christians. Much like the evangelistic programs Evangelism Explosion and FAITH Evangelism for Christians, atheists have books and videos tailor-made for propagating the message of naturalism. I'm guessing they won't co-opt the title *soul winners* for their skeptic missionaries, though.

In his book *A Manual for Creating Atheists*, Peter Boghossian describes the optimal evangelist for deconverting Christians: "Enter the Street Epistemologist: an articulate, clear, helpful voice with an unremitting desire to help people overcome their faith and to create a better world."[6] The author uses the term *epistemologist* to describe a person who helps others determine what constitutes true knowledge—which is to be found, he suggests, in atheism. In other words, a worldview that begins with something other than nature, like Christianity, cannot provide true knowledge. Such knowledge can only be found by beginning with a God-free cosmos.

That's why Boghossian encourages atheists to invite their Christian friends into "a world that uses intelligence, reason, rationality, thoughtfulness, ingenuity, sincerity, science, and kindness to build the future."[7] Such a view is contrasted with Christianity, which is said to be "built on faith, delusion, pretending, religion, fear, pseudoscience, superstition, or a certainty achieved by keeping people in a stupor that makes them pawns of unseen forces because they're terrified."[8] You can't argue with a thoughtful and kind worldview versus a perspective built on delusion.

Another book with a similar theme of godless evangelism is *50 Simple Questions for Every Christian*, by Guy P. Harrison. The questions are intended to displace confidence in the Christian message. The first question, "Does this religion make sense?" is also the guiding inquiry of my book.[9] It's a question that hits home with Thomas. He must decide, "Am I sufficiently convinced to call myself a Christian?"

This summarizes Thomas's mission in the face of Zach's challenge. A challenge that launches an authentic conversation about faith between friends. A challenge ripe with opportunities.

What's the Matter?

This reminds me of the exchange between Richard Dawkins and David Robertson, a pastor in Scotland. Their letters are published in the short paperback *The Dawkins Letters: Challenging Atheist Myths*. The correspondence began when Robertson responded to Dawkins's book *The God Delusion*.

I found their dialogue both entertaining and helpful, but one particular point stood out. After the exchange with Dawkins, Robertson began to hear from readers, many of whom were atheists. Robertson found many of these conversations insightful, but they almost always ended up going back to respective presuppositions, things we assume but cannot prove about reality.

I've found this to be true myself. My best conversations with atheist friends have dramatized how our contrasting starting points control where we end up. It's like we're on open escalators going in opposite directions. We can talk to each other up to a point and appeal to each other to come along with us. But we're up against the reality that we've taken our stances on different starting points leading to different places.

Presuppositions are like the ground we stand on or the track we take. They allow outcomes, frame vantage points, build worldviews. They control what we find thinkable and believable, and whether we're willing to "go there."

Central to Thomas's assumptions about reality is a belief in the existence of an eternal and personal Creator. This is his starting point for making sense of the world. Zach, on the other hand, begins with nature as his fundamental presupposition: nature is all there is. For Thomas reality is described by Christ; for Zach, by chance or chaos.

As an atheist now, Zach certainly no longer believes in

God. He's comfortable with the idea that the cosmos is all there is, or ever was, or ever will be. He believes that the material stuff making up the cosmos is all that's real.

But what exactly is this material stuff that makes up the universe? What must an atheist assume about this ultimate reality?

A few centuries before Jesus was born, a Greek philosopher named Democritus took a stab at describing this very thing. He believed atoms are the basic building blocks that make up everything we see and correspondingly all that is. He considered atoms indivisible. The word *atom* itself means "that which cannot be cut or divided."

The term comes from two Greek words: *tomos* means cut, and the letter *a* in front is a negation.[10] The word *atheist* is formed the same way: the *a* simply negates *theos*, the Greek word for God, giving us literally "no God." Many believe Democritus was both an atomist and an atheist. And according to the late atheistic author Victor Stinger, atomism equals atheism. If all that exists is the stuff that makes up the natural world, then there is certainly no room for God.

Depending on what you thought of his atomism and atheism, Democritus could be a fun guy to have around. In fact, his nickname was the "Laughing Philosopher." If you were to go back in time to the 300s BC, you might find him at the center of social life somewhere in Athens mixing it up at a toga party and poking fun at human folly. But if you fast-forward over twenty centuries to our day, what do modern-day atheists believe about the building blocks of reality?

For starters, we now know that the atom can be divided, a scientific breakthrough with serious consequences, considering the death toll of Hiroshima and Nagasaki. What about the consequences of an atheistic view of matter?

Three things would be hard to avoid while retaining an atheistic outlook. On the assumption of atheism, it seems that matter must be eternal, impersonal, and nonrational or mindless. This would seem to flow from the atheist's basic understanding of ultimate reality.

First, *matter would have to be eternal*. Lawrence Krauss, an atheistic author and theoretical physicist, has recently suggested that the universe came from nothing. If his book, aptly named *A Universe from Nothing*, solved the philosophical riddle of why there is something instead of nothing—as Richard Dawkins boldly claimed in his endorsement—then this would prove that matter is *not* eternal. It came from nothing.

Krauss admits in his writing and speaking, however, that the "nothing" he refers to isn't really *nothing*, at least not the way we conventionally understand the term. He describes nothing as a "bubbling, broiling, brew of virtual particles."[11] He also admits that he cannot account for the physical laws that guide the nothing.

If the "nothing" Krauss is referring to includes preexisting matter, energy, or laws, then he doesn't really explain how the universe came from nothing. Instead, he is simply theorizing about how the universe came from *something* (virtual particles and physical laws). Of course this would certainly make for a less provocative book title: *A Universe from Something*. It would also imply that this preexisting something—if not created—has been around forever.

Second, *matter would have to be impersonal*. Take away a personal Creator, and you have no way to account for persons within the cosmos. On the other hand, if you have an eternal, personal, intentional force behind the creation, you no longer have atheism. It's one or the other—a personal Creator who gives the universe and its occupants a purpose and values, or eternal stuff that is impersonal and just there. If anything that makes up the cosmos qualifies as personal, purposeful, guided, or good, then you have taken a big step away from naturalism.

This dilemma can be seen clearly in an excerpt from Richard Dawkins's book *River out of Eden: A Darwinian View of Life*:

> In a universe of blind physical forces and genetic replication, some people are going to get hurt, other people are going to get lucky, and you won't find any rhyme or reason in it, nor any justice. The universe that we observe has precisely the properties we should expect if there is, at bottom, no design, no purpose, no evil and no good, nothing but blind, pitiless indifference.[12]

Finally, *matter would have to be nonrational*. You cannot hold to atheism and still have a mind as the source

Christ or Chaos

of all things or reasonable minds as part of the world of matter. This creates a pretty big obstacle for atheist intellectuals who are willing to consider it. The prolific author and Notre Dame University professor Alvin Plantinga has spilled a fair bit of ink on this topic in what he describes as the "The Evolutionary Argument against Naturalism."[13]

At the risk of oversimplification, let me summarize: Plantinga essentially argues that eternal, impersonal, and mindless matter cannot provide a proper foundation for proving that our minds are reliable. If our brains are just one more accident in a long string of accidents that have led to the world we live in, then why should we trust what we think? Our brains are mindless outcomes. If we are the products of unguided evolution, then there is no reason to consider our brains trustworthy. We can say they are directed at survival, but that isn't necessarily the same thing as being directed at truth or justice. (I'll say more about this in chapter 5.)

The simplest way around this problem is to insert some kind of mind behind the creation of the world that initiates and guides the process. But if you make this move, you have taken a giant leap away from atheism. Thomas Nagel, an atheist and well-known philosophy professor at NYU, flirts with this notion in his 2012 book *Mind and Cosmos: Why the Materialist Neo-Darwinian Conception of Nature Is Almost Certainly False* (Oxford University Press). He ponders that there must be more behind reality than just eternal, impersonal, and nonrational matter. He just doesn't come to any clear conclusions as to what it must be.

So, in sum, atheist presuppositions begin with eternal, impersonal, and mindless matter. These presuppositions must be taken on faith and cannot be proved scientifically.

Atheism is irrational—that at least is how one atheistic philosophy professor, Crispin Sartwell, describes his God-free worldview in a 2014 article published in *The Atlantic*:

> Ironically, this is similar to the totalizing worldview of religion—neither can be shown to be true or false by science, or indeed by any rational technique. Whether theistic or atheistic, they are all matters of faith, stances taken up by tiny creatures in an infinitely rich environment.[14]

Crispin's honesty is shocking. He says he has taken "a leap of atheist faith" by committing to a view of the universe as a natural and material system. And he says other atheists should own up to their faith commitments as well by calling for an atheism that displays epistemological courage.

The notion that believers rely on emotions while atheists form their worldview through rationality is simply false, Crispin says. Both require a "bold intellectual commitment" that cannot be proved with scientific data. In this way, Crispin concedes that his atheism is more of an interpretation and less of an argument.

And that's where Thomas and Zach's conflict really lies,

with interpretations and presuppositions. The atheist novel begins with an interpretation, a bold intellectual commitment to a view of the natural universe resulting from eternal, impersonal, and mindless matter. That really seems to be what the late Carl Sagan, atheistic scientist from Harvard University, implied many years ago when he famously said, "The cosmos is all that is, or ever was, or ever will be."

But is *cosmos* the best word to describe Sagan's view of reality? Would not *chaos* better summarize a narrative that begins as an accident and is governed by blind chance? It seems the atheist is forced to build every subsequent chapter of his or her worldview novel on an introduction that begins with mindless forces, is governed by nothing, and is going nowhere.

On Losing Oneself

A number of atheists recognize that this starting point might not support everyday human values. Or rather, that many things we highly esteem are actually illusions. The premium we place on our minds to discover truth is one example. Other values seem difficult to reconcile with an atheistic worldview.

As an atheist himself, Duke University philosophy professor Alex Rosenberg suggests in *The Atheist's Guide to Reality: Enjoying Life without Illusions* that things like personhood, human significance, and the ability to make meaningful decisions and moral distinctions are all illusions. His conclusions seem in keeping with the notion that everything stems from eternal, impersonal, and mindless matter.

The question readers should ask is whether you can build a rational bridge from matter and chance to human values like free will and morality. Can you get there from here? Rosenberg says no.

Rosenberg's mantra throughout the book is that the facts of the physical universe are what fix the facts of the human experience. This makes sense if the physical is all that is, or ever was, or ever will be. If all that exists is the material universe and physical laws, then the only things we should treat as facts are what we can discover through physical science.

The only problem with Rosenberg's premise is that it's wrong. Or to be more specific, it's self-refuting. The statement "physics fixes all the facts"[15] isn't itself a physically verifiable fact. In other words, he says we should accept only physical facts while, it seems, he's hoping we don't notice the one glaring exception to this rule: the very thesis statement undergirding his entire project. He seems to overlook this altogether nonphysical assumption.

The reason Rosenberg's claim can't stand up to its own test is that it's a philosophical value, not a scientific one. For "physics fixes the facts" to be a fact itself, we must be able to discover it through physical science. But science cannot do that. We won't discover it under a microscope or through a telescope. It is an assumption the atheist must make about the world, an assumption that the physical world is all there is, or ever was, or ever will be.

And what if this assumption is wrong?

This is not to imply that all atheists think it's impossible to explain the nonphysical. In his little book *Atheism: A Very Short Introduction*, Julian Baggini, an atheistic philosopher, gives this defense: "What most atheists do believe is that although there is only one kind of stuff in the universe and it is physical, out of this stuff comes minds, beauty, emotions, moral values—in short the full gamut of phenomena that give richness to human life."[16]

So, atheism doesn't necessarily require you to reject nonphysical things like beauty and morality according to Baggini. Or at least that's what he says in his short book on atheism. But he seems less hopeful in his 2011 TED talk "Is There a Real You?" delivered to high school students.

In this talk Baggini grapples with the implications of how this "one kind of physical stuff in the universe" relates to our idea that humans have personhood, the notion that we are selves. He says:

> There isn't actually a "you" at the heart of all of these experiences. . . . You are the sum of your parts. . . . If everything else in the universe is like this, why are we different? Why think of ourselves as somehow not just being a collection of all our parts, but somehow being a separate, permanent entity which has all those parts?[17]

Is there a real you? Baggini asks. And his response is essentially, "Not really."

These examples illustrate some reasons why Thomas

isn't convinced that Zach is right. Eternal, impersonal, and mindless matter doesn't seem to offer a compelling explanation for what it means to be human. Thomas isn't ready to take Rosenberg's advice and reject the human experience as fiction by discarding things like free will and moral distinctions. Or Baggini's verdict that we are no more than the sum of our physical parts.

A Literary Loop

This clash between religious and secular worldviews is certainly not new. The celebrated science fiction author H. G. Wells also dipped his pen into the genre of historical narrative in an attempt to explain humanity without reference to religion. His book *The Outline of History*, published in 1920, sold over two million copies and has been translated into multiple languages. He described this massive tome as "an attempt to tell, truly and clearly, in one continuous narrative, the whole story of life and mankind so far as it is known to-day."[18]

Wells brought his skill as a wordsmith and his philosophically nuanced perspective as a skeptic fully to bear on the project. The impact of the Wellsian worldview is illustrated in the true story of a young Jewish father in New York City who required his eight-year-old daughter, an intellectual prodigy, to read the work in its entirety, resulting in her conversion to atheism.[19] But the book was not without its challengers.

Just a couple of years later, back in Britain, an opinionated journalist took up the task of countering Wells's manifesto with a book of his own. The author was G. K. Chesterton, and the book was *The Everlasting Man*, which I quoted at the beginning of this chapter. Chesterton challenged Wells's premise that atheism offers a more compelling account of history. Chesterton contended that Wells's main problem in the book was simply that he was wrong.

The then atheist professor C. S. Lewis read Chesterton's *Everlasting Man* in the mid-1920s and later described the book as a major contribution to his trajectory away from atheism and his conversion to theism. In the following years, Lewis moved from theism into the thing itself, the gospel of Jesus Christ. This propelled him onto an international platform for defending his faith during a time of war.

Lewis's keen mind and clear prose providentially reached that same household in the Bronx where Wells's book had left its mark years before. The aforementioned young girl, now a grown woman, was jolted by Lewis's clear presentation of the gospel, which led her to begin reading the New Testament, a surprising activity for a Jewish atheist. Even more surprising, she went on to reject atheism, like Lewis years earlier, and embraced the offer of the gospel.[20]

Her name was Helen Davidman. That name might sound familiar to you. She later moved to England and subsequently became the wife of C. S. Lewis, bringing the literary loop full circle.

The contrast between Wells's *Outline* and Chesterton's *Everlasting Man* illustrates the fundamental difference between Zach's and Thomas's perspectives. It's a matter of which interpretation, which bold intellectual commitment, accounts for the human experience.

Hypothetically, both could be wrong in their views regarding ultimate reality. Yet one thing is certain: they cannot both be right. And it seems their respective worldviews represent two of the most widely held belief systems in Western culture.

Thomas has decided to begin his response to Zach's challenge that Christianity is irrational by reflecting on the opening chapters of Genesis. What insights, if any, does the Bible offer for explaining the origin of the cosmos?

To answer that, we must head back to the beginning.

2

The Cosmic Song

If the whole universe has no meaning, we should never have found out that it has no meaning: just as, if there were no light in the universe and therefore no creatures with eyes, we should never know it was dark. *Dark* would be without meaning.

C. S. Lewis, *Mere Christianity*

Thomas has decided to begin with the beginning. And he knows that, as in a Choose Your Own Adventure book, the first move has massive implications. Thomas wants to give serious consideration to whether Christianity explains reality as we live it. He wants to know if starting with the Christian account of origins, instead of with eternal, impersonal, and mindless matter, will lead to a convincing view of reality.

While the age of the earth is a point of heated debate in some Christian circles, that really isn't Thomas's specific concern. He's much more interested in which account—Christianity or atheism—has provided a consistent explanation of origins. So he's focused his attention on this point in time—or better yet, the moment before time began—to contrast the two worldviews.

There are loud voices on both sides of the equation, but there is no physical evidence that can conclusively prove either position. There are a lot of theories—some better than others, some that seem to match our lived experiences more or less—but there's no smoking gun to seal the deal. Any position regarding origins requires faith. It is a fundamental commitment you must make apart from evidence, as mentioned in the last chapter.

And any theory that involves the universe coming into existence at a point in the finite past always includes, either consciously or subconsciously, a view of ultimate reality that entails what brought the universe into existence. Behind every theory is an assumption of what existed before time. There is a "pre-beginning" commitment behind every account of the beginning. Even children's books take sides.

I think of my kids' Berenstain Bears book collection. For the record, I'd put their small library up against any other kids' in the neighborhood. But the largest Bears book on their shelves contains the biggest controversy. It's *The Berenstain Bears' Big Book of Science and Nature*. One chapter begins with these words, speaking of nature: "It's all that is or was or ever will be!"[1]

Sound familiar?

It's a paraphrase of Carl Sagan's opening line from the documentary *Cosmos* that I quoted in the previous chapter. Though the newer Berenstain Bears books are now punctuated with religious themes, this earlier work illustrates the intellectual landmines surrounding statements about ultimate reality. If nature is all there is, or ever was, or ever will be, then there is no room for a Creator.

While Sagan's declaration sounds terribly scientific, it isn't something that can be substantiated through scientific experimentation. It's a faith claim. This is the first twist in the plot of the "choose your own adventure" story.

G. K. Chesterton once compared an open mind to an open mouth. His point was that an open mouth is intended to close on something solid. You cannot evade forming a position forever. In the same way, while the origin of the universe cannot be proved scientifically, it's not something a person can really remain indifferent to indefinitely. We might have to make an informed assumption just to get past the first page of our worldview story.

On Making Assumptions

We all make basic assumptions all the time. In fact, there are some things you must assume just to start your day. For example, you cannot prove that there are other minds in the world. Everyone else could very well be a figment of your imagination. Sound crazy? It's actually true.

You cannot conclusively demonstrate that there are other minds because all your proofs could also be more mental creations. Some people actually hold this view, known as *solipsism*. As one philosopher has quipped, you shouldn't make people who hold this view angry. Since we're figments of their imaginations, if they get mad and leave, we're all going with them!

Hollywood plays on these themes with movies like *The Matrix*. For example, you can't prove you're not a brain in a vat connected to a super computer in the lab of an evil scientist. Every example you give to counter this could just be a false impression he is programming into your mind. Creepy, isn't it?

Another often cited example is that you cannot prove that history is real. Perhaps the entire universe came into existence only a moment ago with all of the physical evidences of age and with a humanity that has a built-in false memory of a past. You can't prove otherwise, beyond all shadow of doubt.

These assumptions, as silly as they might sound, are ones we make about the world around us every day. We assume that there are other minds, that we are not brains in vats, and that the past is real. You can get a headache thinking about this stuff, but these are the kinds of things we assume just to get out of bed every morning. And like these examples, we have to presuppose why there's something rather than nothing, where it all came from, and why there's something awfully significant about us all.

Einstein's Error

This reminds me of the NASA scientist Robert Jastrow, a self-professed agnostic who believed that science's inability to lift the curtain on the origin of all things is itself evidence that there's more to reality than nature. In his book *God and the Astronomers*, he highlights the surprise of many scientists in the late sixties and early seventies at the evidence that the cosmos had a beginning. Prior to this evidence, it was widely held that the universe was eternal.

When research seemed to point the other way, Jastrow notes, the response of many scientists was not intellectual but emotional. "It turns out that the scientist behaves the way the rest of us do when our beliefs are in conflict with the evidence," Jastrow writes. "We become irritated, we pretend the conflict does not exist, or we paper it over with meaningless phrases."[2] And though Jastrow doesn't subscribe to any religious position, he doesn't adopt a rigid naturalism either.

Jastrow draws attention to a controversy involving one of the all-time greats of science, Albert Einstein. When Einstein published his general theory of relativity, he didn't seem comfortable accepting one of the most significant implications of his genius accomplishment. A Russian mathematician named Alexander Friedmann discovered that Einstein had made a simple mistake in algebra, which limited his conclusions.[3] But Einstein didn't receive the correction from this junior scientist very well. When Friedmann's analysis was published in a professional journal, Einstein was forced to send a reply. Unfortunately for Einstein, his response included the same error.[4] To Einstein's credit, he later recognized his error and gave Friedmann proper credit. But why the initial resistance?

Friedmann's solution to Einstein's equation demonstrated how the general theory of relativity points toward an expanding universe, suggesting a beginning of time and space. Einstein initially considered such a position "suspect" and rejected theories about an expanding universe, saying they were irritating and that to admit such a possibility "seems senseless."

But Friedmann carved out his place in the science hall of fame as the man who fixed Einstein's math and contributed to an understanding of the universe as having a beginning, evidenced by its expansion. Friedmann's biographers summarize his accomplishments in a book whose subtitle dubs him *The Man Who Made the Universe Expand*:

> Friedmann is seen as a profound, independent-minded, and daring thinker who destroys scientific prejudices, myths and dogmas; his intellect sees what others do not see, and will not see what others believe to be obvious but for which there are no grounds in reality. He rejects the centuries-old tradition which chose, prior to any experience, to consider the Universe eternal

and eternally immutable. He accomplishes a genuine revolution in science. As Copernicus made the Earth go round the Sun, so Friedmann made the Universe expand.[5]

Friedmann was willing to swim against the intellectual current of his day by suggesting an alternative position. Scientists are now able to see what is called the red shifting of planets, offering additional proof of Friedmann's controversial claim that the universe is expanding. This debate illustrates how dearly we hold to our presuppositions about reality.

Still, behind the explosive event of our universe's origin is the mystery of what was there only moments before. And the logical options seem to be limited to either nature or something outside of nature.

I remember watching a debate between an atheistic philosopher and a Christian apologist when this topic came up. The apologist asked, "What would we find if we could see beyond nature?" The atheist responded, "It's obvious, we would find more nature." But why is that obvious? Apparently the philosopher was unwilling to reconsider his assumption that nature is all there is. But what if there *is* more?

Thomas too is being asked to question his assumptions. But is there such a thing as open-minded uncertainty? Should Thomas become agnostic about the origin of the cosmos?

Cosmic Crime Scene Investigation

While there is no smoking gun that can prove with absolute certainty the cause of the cosmos, a "crime scene" as big as the universe itself is littered with evidence.

If you've ever seen the popular show *CSI* (*Crime Scene Investigation*), then you surely have seen cases that involve gun shot residue. Forensic science can help identify whether a person has fired a weapon.

When someone pulls the trigger of a gun, the firing pin impacts the shock-sensitive primer that ignites gunpowder, creating an explosion and forcing the bullet down the barrel. Metals within the primer are vaporized from the heat and escape from the weapon, then quickly cool and settle on whatever is close by. Whoever is handling the gun when it goes off will inevitably have dried residue on their hands and clothing. And police officers can then detect this residue and help identify the shooter.

It's always amusing to see some guy on *CSI* who adamantly denies firing the weapon. When his shirt is sent off to the forensics lab, the results are conclusive: he's the shooter.

The universe is kind of like this, in that there is residue left over from the creation event. But who was the shooter?

A group of scientists at Princeton University actually predicted that if the universe is not eternal, there will be physical evidence of the fact, something not dissimilar to gun shot residue. But before they could test their hypothesis, two scientists serendipitously beat them to the punch in the mid-1960s. Arno Penzias and Robert Wilson discovered low-level "noise" or interference when pointing a sensitive horn antenna toward the sky. After exhausting other possibilities, they concluded that it had to be coming from space.

Years later, in 1978, both men were awarded a Nobel Prize for their discovery of what is now called cosmic microwave background radiation. This radiation is what is left over from what scientists call the Big Bang. In other words, it is evidence of the creation event.

You've probably experienced evidence of this radiation at some point in your life. I remember when cable television had a bedtime. It was around midnight. I would often stay up late and watch reruns of the old black-and-white sitcom *The Honeymooners*. After the show ended, the network would show an American flag, play the National Anthem, and then broadcasting would take the rest of the night off. Literally.

When the programming would end, the screen would just show speckles and make a noise like a walkie-talkie when no one is talking: *kssssshhhhhh*. Scientists estimate that between 1 and 10 percent of the interference that makes the electrical noise, or "snow," on the television is caused from the cosmic microwave background radiation.

Even the walkie-talkie noise is, in part, caused by the same radiation. It's everywhere! That means when you see a screen doing this or you hear the interference on a walkie-talkie, you are witnessing physical evidence left behind from the creation of the universe. That's pretty mind-blowing, in my opinion.

But Thomas must ask whether this really proves the biblical doctrine of creation. Does the new idea support the old idea? Does it show there was a creative beginning?

As we saw with Einstein, the idea of a universe that is not eternal wasn't accepted until fairly recently in the history of science. Going all the way back to the philosophical giant Aristotle, an eternal universe had been the prevailing view. To their credit, scientists like Einstein, though somewhat begrudgingly, adjusted their views to match the evidence. But the Bible never had to realign with the evidence. For thousands of years it has declared, "In the beginning."

Richard Dawkins, however, claims that religion offers no insights into the real world. "You can see that they [religions]," he says, "don't contain any of the knowledge that science has patiently worked out."[6] But is this really the case? Does Christianity offer no knowledge that lines up with what science has worked out?

The title of a *New York Times* article by Malcolm Browne seems to suggest otherwise. The article "Clues to the Universe's Origin Expected" features an interview with Arno Penzias from 1978, shortly after he received the Nobel Prize for his codiscovery of cosmic background radiation.

Browne recounts, "'My argument,' Dr. Penzias concluded, 'is that the best data we have are exactly what I would have predicted, had I nothing to go on but the five books of Moses, the Psalms, the Bible as a whole.'"[7] This award-winning scientist made no bones about it: the Bible clearly predicted this sort of thing a long time ago. From what Dr. Penzias found as a scientist, there is physical evidence confirming a beginning that he would have expected had he nothing to go on but the Bible, even though centuries of thinkers held that the universe was eternal.

This reminds me of a debate between Richard Dawkins and Oxford University professor and Christian apologist John Lennox. Lennox cited this same example of the Bible providing predictive value regarding the universe's beginning. Dawkins flippantly replied that it's a fifty-fifty chance; either the universe did or did not have a beginning. In other words, the odds of guessing right are pretty good. While Lennox conceded this point, he also reminded Dawkins that it was Christianity, not atheism, that had been on the right side of the issue literally from the very beginning.

But might the universe offer us a hint as to what brought it into existence? What can we go on when forming our bold intellectual commitment regarding the nature of the universe? Must we take a blind leap of faith, whether atheistic or theistic? Or are there clues to what lies beyond, if anything at all?

3

The Major Anthem

We do not want merely to *see* beauty. . . .
We want something else which can hardly be
put into words—to be united with the beauty
we see, to pass into it, to receive it into ourselves, to bathe in it, to become part of it.

C. S. Lewis, *The Weight of Glory*

To Thomas the cosmos is telling an ancient story, a primal creed. That's part of what distinguishes cosmos from chaos in the Christian framework. The ebb and flow of human history seems to be governed by a moral compass, just as the gravitational pull of the sun and moon controls the tide. And this splendor and goodness in the world appears to defy scientific explanation.

This tangible mixture of artistic and moral beauty

woven into the fabric of the universe implies a powerful and personal source. It seems nearly impossible to Thomas that it could all be explained as mere products of time and chance. The heavens seem to be sending a very different message.

Many years ago our family vacationed with my mom's family in the Upper Peninsula of Michigan. I used to love our annual northern journeys there to visit aunts, uncles, and a multitude of my cousins. Our trips usually began the same way. My parents would wake my older brother and sister and me in the middle of the night. We would stagger out to the car like zombies and collapse into the back of our small hatchback, which was loaded to the gills and burdened with a well-worn travel bag tied on top.

We would sleep for the first few hours, bumping back and forth into one another like crash dummies in slo-mo. The sun would just be coming up as we neared Chicago with its skyscrapers silhouetted against a glow of pink and orange. We would weave our way through the woodlands of Wisconsin and always stop and buy cheese at a small family-owned store just north of Green Bay.

From there our trip turned from interstates into two-lane highways through small towns with odd names. Excitement would build when we crossed the Michigan state line. And it was clear we had arrived when we turned onto a gravel road that led through tall pine trees and opened to a panoramic view of Lake Michigamme, the reservoir of some of my fondest childhood memories.

I remember one time I took a canoe out late on a moonless night. Both the sky and the lake were deep black. The dark canopy overhead was speckled with bright stars that reflected on the calm water below. It was hard to tell where the sky ended and the lake began. I don't think I've ever been more in awe of nature. I vividly recall a sense of true wonder. And it made me think about the goodness of God.

God's Broadcasting Station

Vacations can free our minds to sense the beauty around us. George Washington Carver once said, "I love to think of nature as unlimited broadcasting stations, through which God speaks to us every day, every hour and every moment of our lives, if we will only tune in and remain so."[1]

Though born into slavery in the state of Missouri, Carver overcame unthinkable obstacles to establish his place as a heroic scientist and inventor. He witnessed firsthand the ugliness of racism and oppression, yet his interpretation of nature's message was never obscured. He believed that nature—even though filled with people capable of great evil—was pointing beyond itself.

Some readers might reject this as sentimental hogwash. But as we saw in the last chapter, the Bible has offered an explanation of the origin of the universe that was confirmed by science in the twentieth century in the face of great resistance. So the claim that Christianity is irrational doesn't seem to hold, at least in regard to the world having a beginning, a subject that science and philosophy had wrong for centuries.

If Christianity is not irrational—if it is indeed a rational explanation of the universe—then Thomas should expect to find insights in the Bible that help him understand both the world and human experience. Could it be that there are elements of the human condition on which science will forever remain mute? Might Christianity speak where science is silent? Can scientists, following the example of George Washington Carver, "tune in"?

The Bible should be big enough to fit in both science and humanity. This is not to say that the Bible is a science textbook. It isn't. Nor is it merely a history book. It's more. It contains history and poetry and instruction and inspiration. It is filled with multiple genres, yet tells one central story.

And this story, the basic plot of the Bible, is what Thomas is contemplating as a guide to reality. But if the Bible provides a consistent explanation of time and space having a beginning in the finite past, why is it that the very mention of a Creator brings such tension and controversy? Why doesn't that evidence seal the deal on there being a Creator?

At the origin of the cosmos, time, space, matter, and energy all came into being. Just based on this, it doesn't seem like a stretch to consider that the source of the universe is eternal (outside time), omnipresent (outside of space), immaterial (outside of matter), and all-powerful (outside of energy). This sounds a lot like the God of the Bible to me. Isn't this a straightforward case that leads the thinking person to accept God's sovereign role in creation?

Nope.

The opposite is often the case. A lot of highly educated people, scientists in particular, don't believe in God. And there is no shortage of theories of origin that reject any sort of supernatural cause, everything from the view that the universe came from nothing (which really is *something*) to the popular notion of a multiverse (for which we have zero physical evidence, and which would merely multiply the puzzle of where everything came from).

A Mixed Message

So why is the origin of the world such contested terrain? It really goes back to our assumptions. There's just no simple way around this. If you assume the natural world is all there is, then you have made a categorical decision. From this starting point you are committed to considering only naturalistic answers. All other alternatives must be rejected out of hand. That's why this approach is categorized as "philosophical naturalism."

I understand how naturalism could clearly seem the more scientific position, but that conviction is not nearly as emotionally neutral as it might sound. Naturalism requires a great deal of faith, beginning with the faith claim that nature is all there is. But Christians interpret the natural world quite differently than naturalists. Both come to the same data, and yet they come away with very different conclusions. Why? The Bible actually speaks to this issue, which sheds a lot of light on the heated nature of much contemporary debate.

Consider Psalm 19, what C. S. Lewis considered the greatest poem in literature. The psalmist states that the heavens declare the glory of God. This means we can tell something of God's might and majesty in the complexity of the cosmos. The heavens speak to us about the power and nature of God.

When you consider the intricate and precise ordering required for our universe to host a planet that allows for intelligent life, you can understand the impetus behind the poem "God's Grandeur," by Gerard Manley Hopkins:

> The world is charged with the grandeur of God.
>   It will flame out, like shining from shook foil;
>   It gathers to a greatness, like the ooze of oil
> Crushed. Why do men then now not reck his rod?
> Generations have trod, have trod, have trod.[2]

The poet is perplexed at how a universe filled with the wonder of God—seeming evidence of his existence found even in the mere fact that the universe itself exists—does not naturally lead men to recognize their Creator. Like the glimmer of light reflecting off of foil, the grandeur of God permeates the world, the poet says, like oil. He then questions why humanity fails to recognize God's abiding power and authority, or as Hopkins says "his rod."

I don't believe there is a simple single answer to this

question. Tim Keller, pastor and author, explains that there are three categories as to why anyone chooses to adopt their particular worldview: rational, personal, and social.[3] Intellectual arguments, social settings and relationships, and emotional experiences all contribute to what we believe to be true about reality. According to Keller, a person's choice is not limited to one category, but a mixture of the three, perhaps with one playing a more pronounced role.

Other categories can be added to Keller's list. Moral autonomy plays a major role for many who reject the existence of God. The title of a book by Christian philosopher James Spiegel illustrates this very point: *The Making of an Atheist: How Immorality Leads to Unbelief.*

We all understand the desire to protect our personal sovereignty. Most of us learned the expression "You're not the boss of me" long before we learned that two plus two equals four. We mastered selfishness long before arithmetic. It's simply in our genes to guard our turf. Even if it is just one square inch of our existence, we want some part of our life where no one is telling us what to do.

The pious reader might cry blasphemy at the preceding sentence. This only illustrates our problem. We all know someone, likely someone close to us, perhaps even ourselves, who would fit each of the following categories: the gluttonous person who doesn't want to hear what the Bible says about moderation, the lustful person who prefers to ignore what the Bible says about purity, or the prideful person content to overlook what Scripture says of humility. It is certain, whether or not the short list fits your particular sin: we all have a tailor-made category that we protect, to our detriment, at all cost. An atheist just goes a step further and applies this to all of life.

The tenth psalm reflects this truth in describing the person who "boasts of the desires of his soul . . . and renounces the LORD" (Ps. 10:3). "There is no God," he says to himself all day long (10:4), but then later finds solace in the contradictory notion that

> God has forgotten,
> > he has hidden his face, he will never see it. (10:11)

This individual pivots between the views that God does not exist (atheism) and that God is not personally involved in creation (deism).

The shifting worldview is a result of the individual hoping he will not be held accountable, a fear that seems just beneath the surface of his daily activities. Worldly pleasures and godless intellectual commitments could be a veneer to cover deeper anxieties. This uneasiness can be temporarily suppressed by believing either that God does not exist or that God is impersonal.

Others fail to connect the created world to a Creator simply because they have never deeply considered these issues. Although moral autonomy can still be a contributing factor, they may suffer from simple ignorance. The apostle Paul explains that faith comes through hearing, and hearing by the Word of God (see Rom. 10:17). But clearly not everyone has heard the Word of God.

Further complicating this matter is the fact that apart from the Spirit of God awakening a sinner's heart, men and women will not comprehend the significance of the gospel message.

That's why our conversations about faith cannot discount the issues of moral autonomy, ignorance, and spiritual blindness, in addition to the categories of intellectual, social, and emotional barriers.

The book of Romans offers insights into this conundrum. "The wrath of God is revealed from heaven against all ungodliness and unrighteousness of men, who by their unrighteousness suppress the truth" (Rom. 1:18). The flip side of Psalm 19, which tells us the heavens reveal God's glory, Romans 1 says that the heavens also reveal wrath. The believer looks up and sees glory. The unbeliever, suppressing glorious truth, sees judgment.

The Cosmic Tapestry

Perhaps that's why pastor and author Doug Wilson says there are two tenets of true atheism: "One: There is no God. Two: I hate Him."[4] The existence of God is not an emotionally or ethically neutral subject. The cosmic tapestry is woven from a moral fabric. The skies are filled with a mixture of glory and wrath, reminding us of a time when our race once knew true good and pointing to a future time when, by holy fiat, goodness will be reestablished through judgment.

In the Genesis account, the days of creation are punctuated with God's declaration "it was good." God told Adam and Eve they could eat freely from all the trees with the exception of "the tree of the knowledge of good and evil" (Gen. 2:16–17). They had no experiential knowledge of evil before their fall into sin. They knew only good.

But since their rebellion, the categories of good and evil have been mingled, and our perception of the two is often blurred. We are tempted to call evil good and vice versa. We are all born in Adam's sin and are in need of a new birth. This is the basic premise of the gospel.

Yet we can still know God's glory in this fallen terrain. Nature still declares the message of goodness, though muffled beneath the blanket of sin's curse. As the apostle Paul explains in Romans 1:18–20, God's divine nature is displayed through the created world. We can know something of what God is like through observation—looking outward at the world and looking inward at the human condition. We are moral beings living in a moral universe. And though science can tell us much about the way the world works, the universality of aesthetic and moral values seems beyond science's explanatory scope.

That's not to diminish the importance of science for understanding the physical world. But there is a sweeter melody to which science as an isolated discipline is hopelessly tone-deaf. There is a goodness that cannot be explained through empirical methods alone. It is the song of the Creator, of his divine nature, broadcast throughout our world. You can sense it in our music, our art, and our acts of kindness.

John Lennox offers a helpful illustration of the limitations of science. He notes that science can tell you if you put strychnine in someone's sweet tea, it will kill him or her.[5] But science cannot tell you that you shouldn't do that. Science can give you an "is," but it cannot give you an "ought." Science is unable to speak into this moral domain, the cosmic tapestry reflecting God's divine nature.

We witness moral and artistic beauty everywhere we go, everywhere we look, yet science, by itself, cannot account for it.

Lest I be misunderstood, I love science. I am deeply thankful for it. Three of my four children have a genetic disease that prevents their bodies from properly breaking down fat. The condition is known as MCAD and is thought to be responsible for some, if not many, cases of sudden infant death syndrome.

My children are able to live mostly normal lives, but they cannot go long periods without a snack. We even have to regulate their sleep to make sure they maintain a regular and steady food intake so their blood sugar levels remain normal. And because they cannot properly break down their own body fat, if they are ever sick and unable to eat, they have to be taken to the emergency room.

I've never once, on any of our trips to our children's

hospital in downtown Louisville, asked our geneticist to treat my kids using only the King James Version of the Bible. That would be pretty silly, wouldn't it? I expect him to know genetics very well, and to help us understand how best to care for our children. Our geneticist actually is a believer, and I'm thankful for that, but that certainly isn't a requirement for treating our children's condition.

This is a good example of the massive benefit of scientific progress. If my children were born in another time, even in recent history, they would likely not have been diagnosed, which could have had fatal implications. So I do love science. But science is not supreme. Science can save my children's lives, but it cannot tell them how to find a life worth living. It cannot give them moral values or purpose.

Think about how much of our lives is deeply impacted by nonscientific values. We cannot give a scientific explanation for beauty or altruism or ethics. But our lives orbit around these realities as the earth revolves around the sun. Why is it so breathtaking to view a vibrant sunrise, or witness a deed of kindness, or hear of an act of heroism? Why do these things strike us with more force than the law of gravity? If they cannot be explained in scientific categories, then why do they seem so important?

Science tells us much. Scripture tells us more. It speaks where science is silent. It can account for the world, and it is big enough still to account for us with all of our wonder and longing and artistic expressions.

Through the Wardrobe

A good illustration can be found in C. S. Lewis's classic *The Chronicles of Narnia*. My favorite Narnia book is *The Magician's Nephew*. And my favorite passage from the book is the creation account of the land of Narnia. The scene is of a small group who have stumbled into a new world filled only with darkness. They fumble about trying to understand where they are until they hear a soft but deep voice.

They stop to listen. They hear singing. Before long a chorus breaks out in perfect harmony, and it seems to Digory, the central character in the story, that the ensemble is made up of the original voice and, oddly enough, that the earth and the newly formed stars and the rising sun are joining the refrain. This is the passage where Digory witnesses the source of the song:

> The earth was of many colours: they were fresh, hot and vivid. They made you feel excited; until you saw the Singer himself, and then you forgot everything else.
>
> It was a Lion. Huge, shaggy, and bright, it stood facing the risen sun. . . .
>
> . . . Then there came a swift flash like fire (but it burnt nobody) either from the sky or from the Lion itself, and every drop of blood tingled in the children's bodies, and the deepest, wildest voice they had ever heard was saying:
>
> "Narnia, Narnia, Narnia, awake. Love. Think. Speak. Be walking trees. Be talking beasts. Be divine waters."[6]

Lewis's touching prose depicts our world too—a world filled with splendor because it is telling a story. It is singing a song, and all of the physical exploration humankind may ever attempt cannot exhaust its glories.

Because its glories are not its own. The heavens declare the glory of God. And deep down we know this to be true. Even if sometimes it takes a story of another world to bring us face-to-face with the reality of our own.

Laura Miller, contemporary author and columnist, confessed that the book that had the most influence on her was Lewis's *The Lion, the Witch and the Wardrobe*. A skeptic, Miller describes the Narnia stories as changing her life. "In one of the most vivid memories from my childhood, nothing happens," Miller writes.[7] This monumental nonevent occurred after she read about the secret passage to Aslan's world. That moment plagued her with a longing to go there in person.

Miller says the Narnia stories spoke to her "across a spectrum of yearning." But in the end, her yearnings are unfulfilled. She concludes, somewhat sadly, that these desires must be illusions:

> Life, unlike stories, has no theme, no formal unity, and (to unbelievers at least) no readily apparent meaning. That's why we want stories. No art form can hope to exactly reproduce the sensations that make up being alive, but that's OK: life, after all, is what we already have. From art, we want something different, something with a shape and a purpose.[8]

For Thomas, however, these stories have power—not because they give us a door into another world, but because they give us a window into our own. The power of story is in offering us a theme, a formal unity, and an apparent meaning for our lives, to use Miller's categories. But most humans live as though these things actually exist. We want them, and we live as though they are real.

That's because God has placed eternity in our hearts. And when we stop long enough to consider what life looks like with the kind of "formal unity" Miller describes, as when we read stories like those about Narnia, something resonates deep inside us. Such stories pull out the innate knowledge that our own world is charged with a greater glory than we have ever imagined. The heavens are singing, and like Aslan's song, we simply want to sing along.

There is something that feels like a sort of force pulling us in this direction, prodding us to live for something greater than nature. It is something we just can't quite seem to put our finger on. Science can't explain it. But we can't deny it. It invades our existence like water seeking its own level. It refuses to be ignored. I think it's the goodness of God. It is his kindness leading us to repentance.

It's a Wonderful World

The world is indeed filled with wonder. All reality reminds us of the goodness of our Creator. And if we search for it, we may find a message of glory. But if we turn a cold shoulder, we will certainly find a message of wrath.

From Thomas's perspective, the Bible makes sense out of mankind's longing for purpose and meaning. We are created in the image of God with intrinsic worth. *Self-evident* is the expression the founding fathers used; it is self-evident that we are created equal. This makes good sense from a Judeo-Christian framework. Other worldviews don't support the idea of the self-evident and intrinsic worth of humans.

Atheism cannot account for such human values. In this regard it seems more irrational for an atheist to live the way most people live, as though things like moral distinctions and beauty are realities. It would seem more rational for the atheist to live consistently with the claim that these things we think so much about and pursue so passionately are mere illusions. But few appear willing to face this grim consequence of their atheism, or to live in light of it.

Perhaps that's because we intuitively know something about the Creator of the cosmos. And we have a difficult time muting this message. It's as though there is a moral code written on our very hearts. We see the world through artistic lenses allowing us to recognize and treasure its beauty, even if there is no one to whom we direct our gratitude.

This goodness around us, and the moral longings within us, are brush strokes left by a divine Artist. Our art is a reflection of his art. Our creativity is a clue that we are made in the image of a Creator. Aslan's song of creation resounds throughout all our songs. We may hear it if we will just tune in.

Consider the popular song from the sixties "What a Wonderful World," performed by Louis Armstrong. It was originally written as an antidote to political and racial tensions. The optimism of the song was intended to offer hope by reflecting on the majesty of nature. But what is it about looking at the greatness of the world that can stir our hearts and imagination even in the midst of unrest?

It is what creation is pointing to beyond itself. Nature is simply doing its job. It is directing our attention upward. It lifts our gaze beyond the problems of our day to a transcendent and personal source. Its tune quietly retells the promise that one day all things will be made new. The heavens declare the glory and wrath of God.

But if the cosmos is indeed charged with the grandeur of God, why is it also filled with such darkness? It is on this point that Thomas and Zach have some of their most tense discussions. Though the problem of evil is nearly as old as time itself, it is as fresh as their most recent conversation.

Does the issue of suffering prove Christianity irrational, or does it fit within the framework of a Christian worldview? And if in the end it's really not a wonderful world, who is to blame—if anyone is to blame at all?

4

The Minor Key

Nature has all the air of a good thing spoiled.

C. S. Lewis, *Miracles*

"You're in good hands." That's what the Allstate Insurance commercials tell us through the deep voice of actor Dennis Haysbert. In one of Allstate's more recent TV spots a child gives this commentary on human tenacity:

> There are man-eating sharks in every ocean. But we still swim. Every second somewhere in the world lightning strikes. But we still play in the rain. Poisonous snakes can be found in 49 of the 50 states. But we still go looking for adventure. A car can crash. A house can crumble. But we still drive. And love coming home. Because I think deep down we know all the bad things that can happen in life, they can't stop us from making our lives good.[1]

The commercial ends with the words on the screen "People live for good." But what exactly is the good? How might we know it, and more importantly, how might we live for it?

Our culture seems to assume the good is real. But is it? Goodness would make perfect sense if the world is the product of a good and powerful source (i.e., the God of the Bible). But can eternal, impersonal, and mindless matter give us a classification for goodness?

The Allstate commercial makes sense only in light of an original goodness intrinsic to the created world. This fits the biblical explanation of the cosmos. It is a theme emphasized in the opening verses of Genesis, where each day of creation is stamped with the words "it was good." But can an unguided world governed by mere chance provide any sort of objective foundation or absolute definition of "the good"? And what exactly is "the good life" if we cannot define the good?

If the world is a product of chance, is governed by nothing, and is heading nowhere, then how can we point to some overarching value of goodness? As the prominent atheistic ethicist Kai Nielsen once said, "We have not been able to show that reason requires the moral point of view. . . . Pure practical reason, even with a good knowledge of the facts, will not take you to morality."[2] And if we cannot get to the moral point of view from a purely scientific perspective, then how can an atheist use a moral point of view to reject the existence of God?

Five Minutes of Hell

Many atheists would disagree with Nielsen's statement. But the real test is whether they can provide an objective foundation for the morality they defend. They may be hanging on—midair, white-knuckled—to a value system that lacks any sort of real grounding. In this way, their values are entirely wishful thinking.

How can there be personal good and evil in an impersonal universe of mere matter and energy? You cannot bracket off your personal experience from reality and claim that you are substantively and qualitatively different from the rest of the world. If the universe doesn't care, then why do you? Either reality is ordered by a moral source, or we are left without categories to call anything truly evil.

Consider two scenes from recent history. In January 2014 a New York–based Satanist group submitted a proposal to build a seven-foot statue of Satan at the state capitol of Oklahoma in protest of a monument of the Ten Commandments displayed there.[3] A spokesperson described the statue as a place of serenity and contemplation where children could sit and find inspiration. I doubt I'm the first to regard the mental picture of this scene as over-the-top creepy.

It should be noted, however, that most Satanists, like the group lobbying for the statue, don't really believe in Satan. Most Satanists are actually atheistic in their outlook, disavowing any spiritual realm. In fact, the group's spokesperson described Satan as a literary construct and made it clear they don't believe in some actual embodiment of evil in the world. They are more or less a political group using Satan as an icon to express their desired secularism.

Now, consider another scene that took place a little over a year prior to the proposal for this statue. Only eleven days before Christmas, twenty children lost their lives at gunpoint in a small northeastern town. On the morning of December 14, 2012, at 9:35, a twenty-year-old man entered Sandy Hook Elementary School in Newtown, Connecticut, and went on a killing rampage before committing suicide at 9:40 a.m.

In the five intervening minutes the horrors of hell were on full display in hallways and classrooms filled with teachers, administrators, and little sons and daughters whose parents would never hold them again, or tuck them in at night, or read them another bedtime story.

Before these precious children left for school that morning, they likely had breakfast with their families in homes warmly decorated for the holidays. There were probably stockings hanging from the mantle and Christmas trees where gifts would never be opened. No one would have guessed that this day would end in bloodshed.

Except for a young man who was busy finalizing his plans and loading his gun.

We all rightly call the act he committed "evil." It was categorically evil. Psychobabble doesn't capture our outrage. And even the most secular among us seem willing to adopt biblical terminology in the face of such an atrocity. Every fiber of our humanity screams "evil," and for good reason.

That's why worldview discussions are not cute intellectual games. We are not playing around. We're confronted with a real question, and it's one every thinking person must consider at some point: *What worldview can account for the human desire to classify certain actions as truly evil?*

To go back to the capitol scenario, imagine if the group had succeeded in building its statue of Satan as a symbol of secularism next to the monument of the Ten Commandments. Two images, two contrasting worldviews. One monument representing a world free from religious explanations, and the other, a world ordered by a moral source. Which of the two gives the ethical framework needed to evaluate the events at Sandy Hook?

The Evil Path That Leads to God

I understand that this is a sensitive issue. There is no way around it. But to reference Kai Nielsen again, if a pure understanding of the facts cannot lead us to the moral point of view, then where does the moral point of view originate? What is the source of our moral values?

We see certain events—cruel, painful, unnecessary events—and we rightly conclude that they are products of evil. But why conclude that? As Richard Dawkins has said, in atheism we should expect to find in the world "no design, no purpose, no evil and no good, nothing but blind, pitiless indifference."[4] If that is true, then why are we morally repulsed when we see scenes on the news of parents lying prostrate in an elementary school yard crying out for news of whether their children have survived?

If there is no design, no purpose, no evil, no good, then why aren't we pitiless and indifferent like the rest of the natural world? In Dawkins's view of the cosmos, the category of evil is lost in a flood of natural negations. We live in an unkind universe that simply doesn't care. And since the word *cosmos* means "a well-ordered system," Dawkins's description misses the mark. *Chaos* would be the more fitting term for the indifferent and pitiless vastness he describes.

But can Christianity fare any better? Can the Christian worldview make sense out of our moral longings? Can the gospel provide a foundation for the good life?

I'll concede this much to Dawkins: our moral instincts lose their meaning if we begin our stories with impersonal causes and fortuitous effects. Whatever time and chance might give us in the natural world, Dawkins is right to point out that they will not give us purpose or moral distinctions. Eternal, impersonal, mindless matter simply doesn't care.

But if there is an intelligent source beyond creation, does that in any way explain both our longings for goodness and our laments of evil? Or does it make things worse? Hasn't

Alex Rosenberg told us, "Reality is rough. But it could have been worse. We could have been faced with reality in all its roughness plus a God who made it that way"?[5] Can we reconcile the existence of God with the presence of suffering?

Blame It on the Rain

Thomas is considering whether Christianity complicates or clarifies the situation historically called the "problem of evil." It is often framed like this: "If God is all-loving, he would want to end evil. If he is all-powerful, he could end evil. But evil still exists. Therefore, either God is not all good, or he is not all-powerful; or he simply doesn't exist."

Thomas realizes, though, that if we remove God from the equation, we find ourselves in the world of Dawkins and Rosenberg, where evil is illusory. If we use evil as a means to shoo God from the cosmic scene, we also shoo away objective moral classifications. The moment God is gone, so go our moral categories, including the very notion of evil, and our right to object to it.

In atheism, our praise or blame of chance rings hollow. Chance cannot be the ultimate explanation and then somehow be held responsible. Chance is impersonal.

Chance is a blind force governing all things, in the atheistic perspective. The world is here by chance. Humans are products of chance. Everything is explained by chance. But chance knows neither rhyme nor reason. It cares not for our pain. It is blind, deaf, and mute. All who hope in chance, hope in vain.

As the poet Steve Turner once penned,

If chance be the Father of all flesh,
disaster is his rainbow in the sky.

Turner goes on to describe violence, theft, and school
bombings and says,

It is but the sound of man worshiping his maker.[6]

If chance is the father of all flesh, then a rainbow of disaster
shouldn't catch us by surprise. And we certainly shouldn't
expect to find a pot of gold at the end.

But if we must keep God in order to retain a category for
our moral judgments, what kind of God are we left with?
What kind of God can sit loftily in the heavens while children around the world lie with swollen stomachs from mal-
nutrition and breathe their final breaths as vultures circle
overhead? What kind of God can watch a disturbed young
man, armed to the teeth, walk into an elementary school
and go on a five-minute shooting spree?

We can't let God off the hook. Christians do believe that
God is all-powerful and all-loving. So does the problem of
evil really render the Christian faith irrational?

As the dean of a Bible College I might be expected to say
I fully understand the complex nature of God's sovereignty
and human accountability. I don't. Scripture presents both
clearly. It doesn't apologize that the two can be difficult
to reconcile. They form a mystery that I won't pretend to

elucidate in such a short work. And I won't claim I could do a much better job in a bigger book.

I've read big books on the subject and still have questions. But I will say—and please hear me clearly—the problem of evil fits well within the Christian framework of creation, fall, redemption, and glorification. Though we cannot assume that an intellectual answer will satisfy such an emotional issue, we also cannot, as Christians, ever forget that the gospel is not undone by human suffering.

That's because the Christian narrative is big enough to fit in the problem of evil. The atheistic story, guided by chance, will forever be incapable of doing so. It must live with an unresolved—or worse yet, unresolvable—tension of experiencing moral longings in a universe void of moral bearings. Only the gospel can afford a rational explanation of moral and natural evil and our innate understanding that these things are real and not illusory.

But the gospel does better still. It offers a remedy.

The gospel presents a God who created the world as perfectly good, and a people who have rebelled against his sovereign rule. This reminds me of an exchange I recently had with my son Micah. "Daddy," he said, "I wish Adam and Eve never disobeyed God." "Me too, buddy—me too," I told him. I love that at such a young age, he is learning to connect the dots between his sin and the sin nature he inherited from the first human, Adam.

This conversation gave me the opportunity to explain to him why the apostle Paul describes Jesus as the "last

Adam" (1 Cor. 15:45). The first Adam should have guarded the garden and protected his bride. But he didn't. The gospel is basically the story of how God came in flesh to do what Adam should have done in the first place. The second or last Adam made things right and promises to one day make all things new.

In the Christian view of history, we are living in the "already" of what Jesus has done, but also in the "not yet" of the new creation. We are between the times, waiting even while we suffer. We live between the two worlds of the old creation, which is fallen, and the new one that is yet to come. Like a child jumping from one rock to another, we are caught in midair while waiting to land.

That's because we see only one frame of this motion picture at a time, but God sees the entire film from beginning to end. And though our suffering might not make perfect sense to us now, at some point in the future it will. We now see through a glass dimly, but one day our vision will be made clear. And at the end of human history, God will not be tried and found wanting.

That's why Christians don't have to adopt an inauthentic disposition and act as though life is a breeze. We must remember that our optimism is forward looking. We smile beneath a *veil of tears*. Our hope is born through grief, for hope is always connected to the future. But the rumor in the New Testament is that one day this hope will be fully realized, and our faith will become sight.

God and Evil

We cannot discount how big a challenge this matter really is. The problem of evil has kept many away from belief in God. One such example is the British philosopher and public intellect C. E. M. Joad.

Joad was outspoken about his agnosticism, due in large part to the problem of evil. His skepticism is evident in an article titled "God and Evil," published in *The Spectator* in January 1941. The following month the magazine published a response to Joad's piece by none other than C. S. Lewis. The two would do more than exchange articles.

Joad turned the theme of the article into a book he published a year later by the same title, *God and Evil*. He references Lewis by name over fifty times in the work.[7] Throughout, he wrestles with Christian responses to the problem of evil, and in the final chapter offers his reasons for rejecting the faith.

A couple of years after the book was published, Lewis invited Joad to discuss it at Oxford University's Socratic Club. It is suspected that Joad spent the night at Lewis's home after the debate, and the two talked late into the evening. It's clear that Lewis made an indelible impact on him. Joad, like Lewis before him, was destined to tread an intellectual road that would eventually culminate in conversion.

In Joad's book *The Recovery of Belief: A Restatement of Christian Philosophy*, he explains his earlier objection to Christianity: "I was for years baffled by the problem of pain and evil; in fact, it was this problem that for years denied belief in the Christian religion."[8] Joad's rejection of the Christian faith because of the problem of evil was not unusual. It is not uncommon even for Christians to doubt the goodness of God because of human suffering.

The real question was, and is, which worldview best explains evil and suffering? The first sentence of Joad's book recounting his conversion tells the whole story: "The following book is an account," he writes, "of some of the reasons which have converted me to the religious view of the universe in its Christian version."[9]

C. E. M. Joad found in the gospel a view of the universe that was capable of answering his questions and explaining his moral impulses. Far from being irrational, Christianity impressed him as the only compelling description of his experiences. Joad exhausted naturalistic explanations and concluded that the answers were to be found elsewhere. "I am here suggesting that just as the explanation of the facts of the natural world must lie outside it, so, too, must the explanation of the facts of moral experience lie beyond it."[10]

For Joad, a naturalistic framework couldn't satisfactorily explain his encounter with the sinfulness in his life specifically and in the world generally. "These doctrines seem to me to cover more of the facts of life than any others [with] which I am acquainted. They make sense of experience and in particular they make sense of its pain and frustration, as no others do."[11] And thus he rejected a naturalistic worldview: "I abandoned it, and in abandoning it found myself a Christian."[12]

Like Joad, Thomas can't help but wonder whose worldview, his or Zach's, is best described as irrational. The fourfold narrative of creation, fall, redemption, and glorification leads him to expect to find both moral and natural evil in the world. These are not anomalies in the Christian narrative; they are central to the plot.

The gospel also informs our understanding of a planet where the vast majority of the people breathing air at this very moment possess some form of religious belief. Conscious of God, good, and evil, they seek ways to resolve life's tensions and mysteries. Christianity leaves room for both suffering and longing. As Lewis once observed, "If I find in myself a desire which no experience in this world can satisfy, the most probable explanation is that I was made for another world."[13]

Even in a world marred by evil, there is enough residual goodness to lift our eyes above the pain. And there we may find peace for our restless souls.

5

Haunted by Transcendence

We may ignore, but we can nowhere evade,
the presence of God. The world is crowded
with him. He walks everywhere incognito.

C. S. Lewis, *Letters to Malcolm*

Thomas doesn't have to convince Zach that most people are religious. This goes without saying. It is patently true and widely evident.

The Bible affirms that part of being human, of being created in the image of God, is having an intrinsic knowledge of God's existence. The apostle Paul shows us in his letter to the Romans that there are two responses to this divine impulse. One is adoration. The other is an active suppression of this truth in unrighteousness, through either hedonism (Romans 1) or humanism (Romans 2).

Does such a claim make sense of the world, or is Paul merely engaged in religious rhetoric? Is this just sectarian sentiment? Perhaps believers are projecting their desire for God onto the world and lumping people into neat categories. Or is it the reverse—that atheists are dispelling belief in God because they fear that it's actually true?

Santa Poisons Everything

I often hear the idea of God compared to Santa Claus. "We all stop believing in Santa Claus at some point in our lives," it is said, "so we might as well discard this childish notion of God while we still have some dignity left."

Yet, behind the story of Santa Claus is a historical person, a fourth-century Catholic bishop named Nicholas, from Asia Minor, remembered for his generosity. And behind the widespread belief in God, perhaps there is something real as well.

But could it be, as with Santa Claus, that we have taken some shred of historical authenticity and woven it into a fabric of festive fiction? The believer should be willing to admit this temptation. The apostle Peter says, "Always [be] prepared to make a defense to anyone who asks you for a reason for the hope that is in you" (1 Pet. 3:15).

On the other hand, the skeptic must give some sort of reason that belief in the divine is so stubborn and prevalent around the world. If it is as silly as belief in a red-suited man climbing down chimneys, then why are there so many religious adults? Belief is resilient. It's hard for our race to eradicate it, even when authors who try to do so dominate the *New York Times* best-seller list.

Belief in God, however defined, appears to be the warp and woof of human cultures throughout history. As James Smith has observed, we seem to be "haunted by transcendence."[1] Like Dorothy in *The Wizard of Oz*, we are wandering down the Yellow Brick Road through a dark forest with a sense of fear and wonder at what might be just around the bend.

The skeptic, who places as much authority in the Darwinian metanarrative as Christians place in the Bible, is not without a ready reply. Religion is merely the product of evolution, a valued resource aiding our species' survival. At some point in the future perhaps we will evolve beyond this need. Some atheistic authors seem to think that this time has already come. But it appears that the global public has missed their memo.

Around the world belief in God holds strong, though secular trends in Western culture have shown an increase in those who opt out of formal religious affiliations. Yet even a large percentage of those who do not affiliate, often called "nones," still believe in the supernatural.[2] So, if we are on the verge of an evolutionary breakthrough resulting in the dissipation of religious belief, the statistics certainly don't show it.

I can hear someone contest, "But that is not how

evolution works. It is slow and gradual. Give it time and belief in God will eventually be left behind." Of course, the naturalist *must* assume that Darwinian evolution will, in time, give an adequate explanation of pretty much everything. For the naturalist, evolution is the only game in town. It is, in essence, the secular religion.

The Evolution of Belief

In a 2011 interview with *The Atlantic* the celebrated sociologist Robert N. Bellah, who taught at Harvard and Berkeley, discussed his newest work, *Religion in Human Evolution*. When asked why he wrote the book, he responded:

> Deep desire to know everything: what the universe is and where we are in it. The meta-narrative that is really the only one intelligible to all well-educated people everywhere in the world is the meta-narrative of evolution, which is in turn embedded in a narrative of cosmological development since 13.7 billion years ago in the Big Bang.[3]

Daniel Dennett, a well-known atheistic philosopher and part of the elite group of new atheists, makes a similar allegation in his book *Breaking the Spell: Religion as a Natural Phenomenon*. Dennett contends that religious belief must be studied scientifically. The form of science he specifically calls for is evolutionary biology. In sum, evolution is responsible for religion, and it is through the study of biology that we will better understand religion's origin.

For the sake of conversation, let's concede this point. Let's assume that religion really is the product of unguided evolution. What might the implications be if this claim is true?

First, it would be clear that religion is false. Religion, at the most basic level, points beyond the natural world. But if nature is indeed all there is, then the religious viewpoint is wrongheaded. In other words, if naturalism is true, then belief in the supernatural is categorically false.

Evolution may have led us to belief in gods, in an after-life, or in some sort of divinely inspired morality in order to provide coping mechanisms that are advantageous to our survival. It's not difficult to imagine how belief in a higher purpose or divine law might help people manage to live together in a tough world without killing each other. But if religion is indeed the result of evolutionary processes, and nothing more, then it is just a helpful, though false, way of seeing the world.

A second implication is that, since most people through-out history have been religious, then evolution, which brought this about, is not primarily concerned with truth. We can say that evolution is focused on survival; that makes perfect sense. But survival and truth are not synonymous. With the majority of people in the world holding a religious perspective of some kind or another, evolution would in-deed be helping people endure, but it is clearly not leading them to a true picture of reality.

False beliefs can sometimes be valuable. For example, it

might be beneficial for a person with a terminal illness to believe she is going to beat the odds. That belief might offer her a measure of courage and hope. Even if, in the end, she isn't victorious, the false belief still is helpful.

Or consider the parent who tells his children they don't need to be afraid when a tornado alarm goes off. With howling winds and shaking tree limbs scraping against the windows, this encouragement might calm them. But the truth is that a tornado alarm is intended to do just that—alarm people. The lie that there's nothing to worry about could help the child in the face of uncertainty, even though it is not entirely true.

Another example is the placebo effect. A placebo is some form of fake medication, like a pill made of sugar, that can have a positive effect on the person taking it. Clinical tests have shown that if a person takes what he thinks is prescription medication, even if it is only a placebo, he often experiences physical benefits.

False beliefs can be our ally in facing difficult times. But when we attribute the false belief of religion to the process of evolution and recognize that the overwhelming percentage of humanity is religious, we are forced to face the fact that evolution, while aimed at survival, is not concerned with truth. Proponents of unguided evolution would have to surmise that at this very moment most people around the world, since they are religious, have a delusional conception of reality.

As a religious believer myself, I'm a card-carrying member of this misled society. And if the religious perspective is a result of unguided evolution, that means evolution is to blame. If evolution is to blame for leading most people to such error, then how can we ever say with any certainty that evolution is concerned with anything more than survival?

The third and final thing we must conclude is that since evolution isn't chiefly concerned with truth, then we should avoid making truth claims based on the evolutionary model. But, you might protest, "We began this whole thought experiment by conceding that it is *true* that religion is a product of evolution!" Exactly. But, as you may have noticed, this final observation calls into question the entire process.

A method that leads the masses to a fundamentally bankrupt view cannot be trusted to give us truth. As the saying goes, "Fool me once, shame on you. Fool me twice, shame on me." How can we implicate evolution with leading the populace to such grave error and then turn around and trust it? It's simple. We can't.

Arthur James Balfour, prime minister of England at the beginning of the twentieth century, made a similar argument in *Theism and Humanism*, cited by C. S. Lewis as one of the books that most impacted his philosophy of life.[4] On the view of unguided evolution Balfour states, "There are no beliefs which do not trace back their origin to causes which are wholly irrational. . . . If Naturalism be true, the causal order is blind."[5]

If the human brain is reduced to atheistic categories that

begin with eternal, impersonal, and irrational matter, then we can never give full confidence to our cognitive faculties. Our brains are accidents and our thoughts are unreliable. Nothing illustrates this more than the claim that religion is the product of evolution. This proposition shows how little we can trust the evolutionary model to lead us to truth.

On this view, the human brain is considered one of the many happy accidents resulting from the Big Bang. Our thoughts are mere by-products of this long string of accidents. In order to avoid this pitfall, some might insert some sort of intelligence or mind behind the process. If there is a rational source behind the world, then our brains could be reliable and our thoughts trustworthy.

That's because if you don't have to trace the origin of your brain back to irrational causes, then perhaps you can establish a basis for considering it trustworthy. But if you make this move, then you have taken a colossal step away from atheism. If the widespread religious perspective is merely a product of evolution—irrational matter plus time and chance—this reveals the low premium placed on truth by unguided evolution.

Is This God?

Belief in the supernatural proves to be an obstinate human characteristic. That's because it is one of our most basic beliefs. It is as though our race was programmed to believe in and yearn for the divine—so much so that the apostle Paul says that the unbeliever must actively and decisively suppress the knowledge of God. That's because the default setting for humans as created in God's image is belief.

History is filled with examples of those who have tried to tamper with their factory settings. But if God is real, as of course I believe he is, then we shouldn't be surprised to discover that he is not sitting idly by while humanity tinkers with its operating system.

Malcolm Muggeridge, the British journalist, author, and media personality, spent most of his life as an outspoken agnostic. Even in his work *The Earnest Atheist*, he took issue with the notion that Christianity could be true "insofar as it fosters beauty."[6] For Muggeridge, Christianity was either true or false. He felt no sympathy for entertaining some intermediate category. And at that point in his life, he had made his choice—he was certainly no Christian.

But his faith in the natural world was shaken on a journey through the mountains in southern India, which he describes in his book *Chronicles of Wasted Time*:

> On my wanderings in the Nilgiris I often caught a glimpse of the plains below; yellow and sizzling, and so far, far away. . . . In this aloofness and remoteness, up there among the fir trees, dark green against a piercingly blue sky, breathing the fresh mountain air, drinking the cool mountain water, bathed in the clear bright mountain sunshine, I had an overwhelming sense of being engaged in a quest. . . . Mulling over this solitary journey afterwards, I had a notion that somehow, besides

questing, I was being pursued. Footsteps padding behind me; a following shadow, a Hound of Heaven, so
near that I could feel the warm breath on my neck. . . .
Some scribbled pencil notes that have survived finish
up with the barely decipherable question: Is this God?
No answer is offered.[7]

Muggeridge may not have understood his experience
at the very moment when he scribbled in his journal, "Is
this God?" But it seems apparent from his reflection on the
event that the obvious answer to the question was yes. It
was God. God was pursuing him. This is clear in his reference to the "Hound of Heaven," the title of a poem by
Francis Thompson about being chased by God.

Muggeridge later said that he "belatedly and reluc-
tantly" came to "see in Christ the only reality in a world
increasingly given over to fantasy."[8] It was the Christian
view of reality that allowed him to understand the real nature of the world. The alternative worldview, the secular
perspective, was fantasy.

As a consummate skeptic himself, Muggeridge came to
Christ not by ignoring questions, but rather by following
them. And he found in Christ something the world could
not offer, as he describes in one of his essays:

Let us remember that it is precisely when every earthly
hope has been explored and found wanting, when every
possibility of help from earthly sources has been sought
and is not forthcoming, when every recourse this world

offers—moral as well as material—has been expended
to no effect, when in the shivering cold the last [bundle
of sticks] has been thrown on the fire and in the deep-
ening darkness every glimmer of light has finally flick-
ered out, that it is then that Christ's hand reaches out
sure and firm, that his light shines brightest, abolishing
darkness.[9]

While the secular moment is certainly *en vogue*, particularly in the West and especially in the academy, can it really
account for what it means to be human? If we abandon
the religious perspective, will we lose what it means to be
human? Could atheism lead to the abolition of man?

Atheists, in claiming that religion is a product of evolution, lose both confidence and credibility in then assert-
ing that anything else is true. Eternal, impersonal, and
mindless matter isn't moving toward anything more than
survival. As C. S. Lewis pointed out, we cannot trust our
thoughts if they are "fully explained as the result of irrational causes."[10]

But we live as though our thoughts are trustworthy. And
most humans live as though God exists. Could it be that
these two values, the trustworthiness of thought and the
religious impulse, are linked? Moreover, could it be that if
you remove the latter, the existence of God, you pull the
rug out from under the former, the reliability of thought?

That's why Thomas sees the idea of God as a reoccur-
ring theme in validating human values. There seems to be

something behind our belief. There seems to be *Someone* behind our religious longing. The Bible even points us to *somewhere* in space and time, a place in the Middle East, where God once left footprints in Palestine.

6

What If God Were One of Us?

Once in our world, a stable had something in
it that was bigger than our whole world.

C. S. Lewis, *The Last Battle*

The secular worldview begins in chance, is governed by
nothing, and is heading nowhere. The Christian worldview
is far better, and to borrow a pet expression from Henry
Kissinger, it has the added advantage of being true. Atheism begins with eternal, impersonal, and mindless matter.
Christianity begins with "In the beginning was the Word
. . . And the Word became flesh" (John 1:1, 14).

The latter statement moves Christianity from the realm
of faith to the sphere of time and space, where mortals

dare to tread with all our big questions, our deep thoughts, and our wandering and wondering to figure out if life has meaning and is worth living. The Christian narrative begins with a metaphysical assertion, "In the beginning was the Word," and moves quickly to a historical claim, "And the Word became flesh." And it is on this singular declaration that Christianity makes itself the most vulnerable of all religions, open to hundreds, nay thousands, of conceivable historical and archaeological negations.

But all these years later, two thousand to be more precise, such negations don't seem to be forthcoming. While Thomas is no expert in archaeology and doesn't have a PhD in ancient Near Eastern history, he knows enough to realize that the Bible has a good deal of historical support and is not easily dismissed. It appears that something profound really did happen some time ago in Palestine. But does the evidence truly point this way?

The highly regarded twentieth-century Jewish archaeologist Nelson Glueck, once featured on the cover of *Time* magazine, certainly thought so. His knowledge of the geography of Palestine was extensive. So much so, that during World War II a United States intelligence agency, known as the Office of Strategic Services, worked with him to develop a tactical retreat plan to evade Nazi troops in Northern Africa. After years of archaeological investigation, Glueck concluded, "As a matter of fact, however, it may be clearly stated categorically that no archeological discovery has ever controverted a single biblical reference."[1]

Some of Glueck's findings, which he said parallel Old Testament passages, were rejected after his death. But more recent research reported in the Proceedings of the National Academy of Sciences has led archaeologists like Thomas Levy to restate Glueck's approach, as the evidence seems again to make relevant "the debate about the historicity of the Hebrew Bible narratives related to this period."[2] Levy, a distinguished professor at the University of San Diego, went on to say, "This research represents a confluence between the archaeological and scientific data and the Bible."

This confluence between biblical accounts and archaeology is the sort of thing one would expect if the biblical story is true. Far from being overturned by evidence, the biblical account garners recurrent and lasting support from scholars. But apart from certain Old Testament stories being verified by archaeologists like Glueck, is there good reason to believe in Jesus?

Aslan and Jesus

I can understand why a skeptic would balk at the claim that there is a God who once visited his creation. Christians shouldn't sneer or be surprised that atheists consider such views laughable. For every book extolling the virtues of the person called Jesus, there seem to be an equal number that demur his character or deny his deity. But are the counter Christian versions better suited to the evidence?

Let's consider one recent book that rocketed to the top of the *New York Times* best-seller list. In his book *Zealot:*

The Life and Times of Jesus of Nazareth, Reza Aslan, an Iranian-American author and professor, challenges the traditional biblical understanding of Jesus. The book captured a great deal of attention, particularly after Aslan discussed it on Fox News with Lauren Green, who began the interview with the question, "Why would you as a Muslim want to write about the founder of Christianity?"

Throughout the interview Aslan repeatedly asserted his credentials as a scholar and professor of religious studies to provide the basis for his work on Jesus. "I am a historian," Aslan said, "I am a PhD in the history of religions."[3] Though the video received attention mainly because of what some perceived to be an inappropriate question by the interviewer, there was perhaps a deeper reason for concern, overlooked by many.

Joe Carter, senior editor for the Acton Institute, points out that Aslan's response was less than forthright.[4] In fact, Aslan does not have a PhD in the history of religions; his terminal degree is in sociology. And he is not a professor of religion, as stated in the interview, but an associate professor of creative writing.

Dale Martin, professor of religious studies at Yale University, made a similar point in his *New York Times* review of Aslan's book: "By profession, Mr. Aslan is not a scholar of ancient Judaism or Christianity. He teaches creative writing. And he is a good writer. 'Zealot' is not innovative or original scholarship, but it makes an entertaining read."[5]

This is not to suggest that Aslan's lack of a terminal degree in religious studies means that he cannot write a book about Jesus. I don't claim to have a terminal degree in apologetics or philosophy, yet here I am, writing this book, which I'm certain will sell fewer copies than Aslan's. However, I do think the discerning reader should take note of Aslan's overzealous presentation of his academic credentials.

One might wonder whether this carelessness shows up in his approach to the life and works of Jesus. And, indeed, it does. As New Testament scholar Greg Carey points out in his *Huffington Post* review of *Zealot*:

> Aslan seems to have bought into an outdated model of Christian development. . . .
> Contemporary scholarship is undermining that familiar model.[6]

And in a review for *Christianity Today*, Craig Evans, distinguished professor of New Testament at Acadia Divinity College in Nova Scotia, gives a similar summary:

> There are numerous problems with *Zealot*, not least the fact that it heavily relies on an outdated and discredited thesis. . . . I cannot help but wonder if Aslan's penchant for creative writing is part of the explanation. Indeed, *Zealot* often reads more like a novel than a work of historical analysis.[7]

While there are a number of factual errors in *Zealot*, I'd like to focus on a particular claim that is easily challenged yet is central to Mr. Aslan's approach to the claims of the

New Testament. He alleges that historical accuracy was of little importance to the biblical writers and their audience.

> The readers of Luke's gospel, like most people in the ancient world, did not make a sharp distinction between myth and reality; the two were intimately tied together in their spiritual experience. That is to say, they were less interested in what actually happened than in what it meant.[8]

It's not hard to see how a young college student sitting in a local bookstore café sipping a cappuccino might find Aslan's writing persuasive. But Aslan is making an observation about the New Testament authorial intent that is at odds with how the biblical authors themselves described their approach.

If they indeed cared little for historical accuracy, this should be evident in what they say and in what they don't say. But the New Testament gives no evidence of a disinterest in history. Its authors were either telling the truth or unknowingly passing along lies, but there is no evidence that they were comfortable mingling the two.

Since Reza Aslan mentioned Luke, the author of Luke and Acts, let's consider his intentions for writing. The Gospel of Luke actually begins with a carefully worded thesis statement:

> Inasmuch as many have undertaken to compile a narrative of the things that have been accomplished among

us, just as those who from the beginning were eyewitnesses and ministers of the word have delivered them
to us, it seemed good to me also, having followed all
things closely for some time past, to write an orderly
account for you, most excellent Theophilus, that you
may have certainty concerning the things you have been
taught. (Luke 1:1–4)

It would seem that Luke is quite concerned with providing a trustworthy account of the life of Jesus. To suggest
otherwise requires us to overlook Luke's clear description.

The apostle Peter, with whom Luke was known to
travel, provides another helpful passage for understanding the biblical authors' approach: "For we did not follow
cleverly devised myths when we made known to you the
power and coming of our Lord Jesus Christ, but we were
eyewitnesses of his majesty" (2 Pet. 1:16). Peter makes a
sharp distinction between myth and historical eyewitness
testimony. To suggest otherwise is to ignore the evidence.

Now, you can argue that both Luke and Peter were
wrong. But what you cannot say—what Aslan had the au-
dacity to say—is that they were comfortable blending myth
with reality. You can claim they misunderstood the significance of the events they described. But you cannot argue
that they didn't care to provide a trustworthy historical
account of Jesus.

Both Luke and Peter eventually died for their teachings
about Jesus. Though martyrdom does not prove truthful-
ness, it is indeed difficult to imagine these men dying for

something they knew to be false. If Peter fabricated his eye-witness account, then why did he not recant at the last moment? Why die for a lie? It's reasonable to maintain that the biblical authors at least believed they were passing down a dependable description of the Messiah.

Compare the work of Aslan with another author who was skeptical of the biblical narrative. Sir William Ramsay was the first professor of classical art and archaeology at Oxford University in 1885.[9] He was knighted in 1906 in recognition of his contribution to academic scholarship.

Ramsay originally approached his archaeological work in Asia Minor with little or no regard for biblical sources. He considered them irrelevant. In fact, Ramsay sounded a lot like Reza Aslan in describing his initial approach to the historical work of Luke:

> His [Luke's] object was not to present a trustworthy picture of facts in the period of about A.D. 50, but to produce a certain effect on his own time by setting forth a carefully coloured account of events and persons of that older period. He wrote for his contemporaries, not for truth.[10]

However, the evidence and the correlating usefulness of the New Testament eventually led to a change of mind and heart. Ramsay later concluded,

> Further study of Acts . . . showed that the book could bear the most minute scrutiny of an authority for the

facts of the Aegean world, and that it was written with sound judgement, skill, art, and perception of the truth as to be a model of historical statement.[11]

Luke is "a great historian," Ramsay later penned, "a writer who set himself to record the facts as they occurred, a strong partisan indeed, but raised above partiality by his perfect confidence that he had only to describe the facts as they occurred."[12] Ramsay came to believe that the Bible provided a reliable guide to archaeological research in the Middle East.

And since the Bible was accurate in those details, he was willing to consider that it might be trusted in other areas as well. That's why Ramsay, who began as a skeptic, will be remembered, among his many achievements and honors, as a compelling defender of the Christian faith.

Christianity: True or False?

But beyond the reliability of the Old Testament affirmed by Nelson Glueck or the trustworthiness of the Gospel narratives promoted by Sir William Ramsay, is it rational to believe Jesus actually rose from the dead? To Zach, this seems like one of the most ridiculous Christian beliefs.

The resurrection is the foundation of the Christian faith and worldview. To deny it is to deny Christianity itself. If the resurrection didn't actually happen, then Christianity is hollow. The apostle Paul makes this point with even more force in 1 Corinthians 15, where he says that if the resurrection of Jesus is not true, then believers are pitiable fools.

I once had a conversation with a well-known Christian author—who will remain unnamed—who rejected the major tenets of orthodox Christianity throughout our dialogue. But the one point he was willing to concede, perhaps merely for the sake of our discussion, was the historical and bodily resurrection of Jesus. Within days of our exchange, however, he published an article that took it all back. He said he couldn't understand the importance or necessity of affirming the actual resurrection of Jesus.

The Bible treats historical claims like the resurrection as decisive and pivotal. They set up Christianity either for confirmation by supporting evidence or for falsification. Events like the incarnation and the resurrection are historically true or they are false. They are not presented as exclusively spiritual realities experienced merely in the hearts of believers. They have their meaning as real events that occurred in real places and at real times.

These events either happened or they did not. Christianity does not enjoy a middle category detached from truth and falsehood. And no amount of spongy liberal rhetoric can undo the implications of the resurrection being historically false. There is no saving Christianity if Jesus did not walk out of the tomb.

But if Jesus actually rose from the dead, his words are forever validated. His resurrection would prove that he is the Messiah, the fulfillment of the Jewish faith. Consequently, his resurrection would prove Islam—a religion developed hundreds of years later—to be patently false, since

Islam teaches that Jesus is not the Son of God and denies the crucifixion and subsequent resurrection.

Jesus's resurrection would also debunk deism, a view that God is not involved in history, since God would clearly have crossed over the mantle of time and space. And Easter, if true, would negate the Eastern religions with their view of an impersonal deity. Finally, if God raised Jesus from the dead, then naturalism would have received its final death blow, forever proving that nature is not all there is, or ever was, or ever will be.

If Jesus rose from the dead, that changes everything. If he didn't, he was a complete sham. The only other option would be that he was delusional. As C. S. Lewis cleverly framed the issue: Jesus was a liar, a lunatic, or indeed Lord of all. But we cannot call him a mere prophet or a good teacher, or use some other nicety fitting something less than a sovereign King. If he rose, he is Lord. If he didn't, he was and is totally irrelevant. There is no middle ground.[13]

Still, I can understand why a skeptic might dismiss this as one more religious claim that can easily be made but never verified. Religious people say crazy things all the time, and unfortunately, given the diversity of religious programming and the advent of the Internet, such wackiness is usually highly accessible.

Thomas must wrestle with whether belief in the resurrection makes sense. Is it just one more crazy claim made by fanatics? Since it is the cornerstone of the Christian faith, it is no surprise that Zach would call Christianity irrational because of it. If the resurrection is false, then Christianity is irrational to the ultimate degree.

Furthermore, Zach has challenged Thomas to consider whether it is possible to prove or disprove that Jesus rose from the dead. If the resurrection is not even subject to proof, might it very well be baseless?

Factually Speaking

This hinges on a particular definition of the word *proof*. If by that we mean something like physical evidence of Jesus exiting the tomb, then clearly we don't have that. There was no antiquarian surveillance camera focused on the stone sealing the burial site of Christ. But that is not the kind of claim that Christians are making. We must pay careful attention to this, because a person's criterion for proof, the sort of evidence required, could reveal a particular bias.

If someone has assumed that nature is all there is, or ever was, or ever will be, then he or she has categorically ruled out the possibility of God's existence, which would necessarily preclude his intervening in history. In other words, the argument could simply be that Christianity is false because naturalism is true. If nature is all that exists, then there is no God, and if there is no God, there is no resurrection.

But this approach demonstrates a fundamental bias and a careless dismissal of the evidence. It's the sort of prejudice illustrated in a statement skeptics often make to Christians, "Extraordinary claims require extraordinary evidence."

While this might sound logical, it's often a way of saying that no amount of evidence could lead the skeptic to accept something supernatural.

If evidence points beyond nature, it is summarily disqualified as never meeting the floating standard of extraordinary evidence. The term is left nebulous, arbitrary, and elusive—conveniently undefined, so that evidence for the resurrection remains always out of reach and unobtainable.

Jim Wallace, a former cold-case detective, describes the way we should approach evidence: "The question is not whether or not we have ideas, opinions, or preexisting points of view; the question is whether or not we will allow these perspectives to prevent us from examining the evidence objectively."[14] In his book *Cold-Case Christianity: A Homicide Detective Investigates the Claims of the Gospels*, he recounts his journey from atheism to Christianity as a result of considering the crucifixion and resurrection of Jesus using cold-case methodologies. The cumulative evidence for the resurrection eventually led to his conversion.

But can we really apply methods of contemporary crime investigations to an event from ancient history like the resurrection of Jesus? Absolutely. History textbooks draw inferences from data much like the inferences made in criminal investigations. As a result, history texts contain numerous examples of events for which we don't have the kind of physical evidence often demanded of the resurrection. So what kind of evidence would be necessary for someone to consider the resurrection?

One method that contemporary Christian scholars have utilized is called the "minimal facts approach," developed by Gary Habermas and Michael Licona. They write, "This approach considers only those data that are so strongly attested historically that they are granted by nearly every scholar who studies the subject, even the rather skeptical ones."[15] These two points, that the data considered is strongly evidenced and that it is widely accepted even among skeptical scholars, form the foundation of their argument.

If you were to consider only the data that meets these parameters, what kind of evidence would Christianity have left? In their book *The Case for the Resurrection of Jesus*, Habermas and Licona outline the following five minimal facts:[16]

1. That Jesus died by crucifixion
2. That the disciples believed that Jesus appeared to them
3. The conversion of the church persecutor Paul
4. The conversion of the skeptic James
5. The empty tomb

Given these five facts, which are both strongly evidenced and widely accepted even by skeptical scholars, what is the best explanation? What would account for the facts of the crucifixion, the disciples' belief that Jesus appeared to them, the conversions of skeptics like Paul and James, and the empty tomb?

This is tricky because, again, there could be unknown or even conscious biases that exclude supernatural explanations from the very beginning. But the discerning reader must consider whether the resurrection of Jesus makes sense out of the minimal facts. One should not disregard these facts and indefinitely evade a conclusion. A decision is afoot.

It is intellectually irresponsible to ignore Jesus. He has made too big a dent in the history of ideas, has staked too audacious claims, and has had too widespread an influence on people to simply be disregarded. But in this short work, I am not foolhardy enough to think I have made a sufficient case for the historicity of the resurrection to satisfy everyone's doubts and questions.

What I do hope is that sincere skeptics might be encouraged to begin with some of the sources mentioned here and to consider for themselves, perhaps for the first time, while attempting to prevent a naturalistic bias from predetermining the conclusion, what explanation really accounts for the minimal facts surrounding the Jewish carpenter from Nazareth who has turned the world upside down.

To Thomas, though not a historian, it seems that Christianity is far from irrational but is rather a reasonable response to facts that are strongly evidenced and widely accepted. Thomas's conclusion can be well illustrated in the words of Jim Wallace:

> If we approach the issue of the resurrection in an unbiased manner . . . we can judge the possible explanations and eliminate those that are unreasonable. The conclusion that Jesus was resurrected (as reported in the Gospels) can be sensibly inferred from the available evidence. The resurrection is reasonable.[17]

Ultimately, it is the Holy Spirit who overcomes biases about what is reasonable, but this does not preclude discussions of the facts of the resurrection. As these discussions echo the biblical narrative, the Spirit works through his Word to change hearts and open minds.

"Duh. Jesus."

This reminds me of a conversation I had with a couple college students at their campus coffee shop. I knew only one of the students well, and I had scheduled a meeting with him to discuss the gospel. He was a quiet kid. I'll just call him Chris. He brought a friend with him for support, whom I'll call Jeff.

Chris had attended several weeks of a Bible study I was leading on his campus. He had expressed interest in the Christian faith but seemed to have some reservations. After we all ordered our caffeine-based beverages and settled in at our table, I kicked things off and tried to get him to open up. Like I said, he was quiet. But his friend was downright chatty.

Jeff, in fact, dominated the conversation. He was a true

skeptic in every sense of the term. His parents were both atheists. He had no formal experience with religious institutions. But he was sincere and quite willing to engage in a meaningful conversation about his questions regarding the existence of God and the Christian faith.

At one point in the dialogue, Jeff began talking about the absurdity of pluralism. With all of the various religions he asked, "Why doesn't God just come down, and say 'this is the one true way'?" I was a little stunned. I didn't anticipate such a helpful set-up question.

I paused momentarily so as not to seem dismissive of his question. If ever there were a perfect pitch for an evangelist to swing at, this was it. But before I could get the bat off my shoulder, Chris, who had been silent all evening, blurted out, "Duh. Jesus." In his short response he summarized the Christian narrative. And in the following weeks he came to embrace the gospel.

There is a religious impulse intrinsic to the human experience that can be validated only by God actually coming down to say, "This is the one true way." That's at the heart of the gospel's claim: the Word became flesh. The incarnation and the resurrection are the historical events from which all of history derives its meaning. All our hope and all our longing is summarized in the simple words of a college student sitting in a coffee shop: "Duh. Jesus."

7

Our Stubborn Smile

The door on which we have been knock-
ing all of our lives will open at last.

C. S. Lewis, "The Weight of Glory"

Human beings are incurably optimistic. We expect to ac-
complish more than our parents, imagine our children will
excel even our exponential generational progress, and anticipate a nice quiet death after a long and fulfilled life. And
I imagine most are betting on a happy afterlife, if they have
any thoughts of an existence beyond the grave. We seem to
think life is going to get better despite all evidence to the
contrary.

In a *Time* magazine article, Tali Sharot writes, "We like
to think of ourselves as rational creatures. . . . But both
neuroscience and social science suggest that we are more

optimistic than realistic."[1] Sharot draws upon research demonstrating that our futuristic target is often set higher than we should reasonably expect to hit, a condition known as optimism bias. Like the downward trajectory of a bullet fired at a distant object, outcomes often fall short of our outlook. But like Charlie Brown in the old *Peanuts* comic strip, we continue to believe that—metaphorically speaking—we'll kick the football this time, or win that baseball game, or talk with the little red-haired girl. At least we can hope.

As one might expect, Sharot chalks up this sanguinity to evolution. "In fact, a growing body of scientific evidence points to the conclusion that optimism may be hardwired by evolution into the human brain." I'm always amazed at all the hardwiring, directing, deciding, and planning attributed to evolution. Somewhere between the Big Bang and the world we live in today, we are supposed to take a massive leap of faith and credit this blind process known as evolution, and its kissing cousin chance, with every kind of intellectual achievement. But I digress.

Despite its advantages for survival, evolutionary optimism is said to be loaded with pitfalls. "Yet optimism," Sharot writes, "is also irrational and can lead to unwanted outcomes." It makes sense that a positive outlook could lead us to over-project and under-protect. For example, while we hope to never experience an earthquake, we had better make sure we are current on our insurance premiums. Our optimism could blind us to reality.

Searching for Someone

But might the optimistic impulse, like the religious one, actually point somewhere? Like the religious outlook, if our optimism is a false view of reality imposed on us by evolution, then how can we break free from the illusion? Should we embrace despair? Must we consider human optimism irrational? Given atheism, I don't see how it can be anything but irrational.

Consider Bertrand Russell's summary of his atheistic perspective in his essay "A Free Man's Worship," included in his book *Why I Am Not a Christian*:

> That man is the product of causes which had no prevision of the end they were achieving; that his origin, his growth, his hopes and fears, his loves and his beliefs, are but the outcome of accidental collocations of atoms; that no fire, no heroism, no intensity of thought and feeling, can preserve an individual life beyond the grave; that all the labors of the ages, all the devotion, all the inspiration, all the noonday brightness of human genius, are destined to extinction in the vast death of the solar system, and that the whole temple of man's achievement must inevitably be buried beneath the debris of a universe in ruins—all these things, if not quite beyond dispute, are yet so nearly certain, that no philosophy which rejects them can hope to stand. Only within the scaffolding of these truths, only on the firm foundation of unyielding despair, can the soul's habitation henceforth be safely built.[2]

According to Russell, humanity is the result of blind causes and purposeless effects destined for extinction. This is where we, according to Russell, must begin if we hope to build a safe habitation for our souls, whatever that might mean.

In his artistic conclusion, it seems he was attempting to open a door to a possible escape. But those who follow his lead will find one set of spiraling stairs after another, leading eventually to a final door that is locked, is double-bolted, and bears a handwritten note that reads, "Better luck next time."

Yet there is a stubborn human habit of living as though we are a part of a better story, something grander, something truly worthy of our lives. It's as though—dark as things look, with rumblings of war, natural disasters, political unrest, economic recession, disease and death—we are holding out hope that someone, somewhere might save the day.

We're waiting for superman. Seriously. Almost all the big-name superheroes grew out of a time of unrest and uncertainty. A CNN article titled "Superheroes Rise in Tough Times" chronicles this phenomenon. Batman, Superman, and Captain America all emerged in the midst of the Great Depression and the early years of World War II.[3]

Our yearning for supernatural intervention can be seen in other historical developments as well. During the Civil War one citizen wrote to Salmon Chase, US Treasury Secretary, asking that the "goddess liberty" be replaced on our currency with a statement of our nation's reliance upon God.[4] Shortly thereafter, the expression "In God We Trust" was imprinted on our coins.

This creed was not added to paper currency until the 1960s, when America was again under extreme duress due to its prolonged military engagement in Vietnam. Similarly, the phrase "one nation under God" was not added to the Pledge of Allegiance until the mid-1950s, which historians link to a growing national concern over the threat of communism, known as the Red Scare.[5]

In times of economic recession, war, and national horror we express our need for divine mediation. In our most vulnerable moments we let the secret out: we really do know of something greater than nature. But this awareness cannot survive in a spiritual vacuum. It is part of the Christian way of viewing the cosmos. It is part and parcel of the Christian narrative.

Pining for a Place

Not only are we longing for *someone*; it seems we are homesick for *somewhere*. And this place is pretty specific, at least according to the highly accomplished biologist and author Edward O. Wilson. In his book *The Meaning of Human Existence* he summarizes the results from a research project that asked men and women to describe the ideal environment in which to live.

"The preferred choice had three factors," Wilson writes. "The ideal vantage point is on a rise looking down, a vista of parkland comprising grassland sprinkled with trees and copses, and proximity to a body of water, whether stream, pond, lake, or ocean."[6] Wilson then introduces the reader to what is known as the African savanna hypothesis, a theory that connects this preferable landscape with our evolutionary origins in Africa. Why do we long for this kind of setting? Wilson's answer is, of course, evolution. How could it be anything else?

Wilson goes on to recount a time he dined at a friend's house in New York City. After the meal they stepped out onto the balcony where there were small potted trees, and a beautiful view overlooking two lakes in Central Park. His friend believed that the human brain at birth is a blank slate without any kind of inherited evolutionary instincts. This would render the African savanna hypothesis meaningless. Wilson ends the chapter by musing on where and how his friend might account for the idea of beauty, if not as a product of evolution hardwired in the makeup of our brains.

I actually think Wilson is onto something. We have a certain view of beauty, a specific longing for place, that seems to us—powerfully at times—to be quite primitive. But I think Wilson stops short. He doesn't go far enough. This picture goes deeper than the African savannas. It points to a time when our race once knew peace.

It is the echo of Eden.

J. R. R. Tolkien described this experience in a letter to his son Christopher:

Certainly there was an Eden on this very unhappy earth. We all long for it, and we are constantly glimpsing it: our whole nature at its best and least corrupted, its gentlest and most humane, is still soaked with the sense of "exile." . . . As far as we can go back the nobler part of the human mind is filled with the thoughts of *sibb*, peace and goodwill, and with the thought of its loss.[7]

This reality was demonstrated recently in the public response to the award-winning motion picture *Avatar*, which portrayed Pandora, an imaginary planet filled with beauty and wonder. Crowds flocked to the new film. But while ticket sales were sky high, the response from fans was surprising.

Many moviegoers shared an experience that was eventually labeled "Post-Avatar Blues," a depression rooted in the realization that Pandora was intangible. Some even described suicidal thoughts when contemplating how drab reality seemed in comparison to the cinematic world. Stephan Lang, one of the actors from the film, responded, "Pandora is a pristine world and there is the synergy between all of the creatures of the planet and I think that strikes a deep chord within people that has a wishfulness and a wistfulness to it."[8]

The movie did strike a deep chord. And I agree with E. O. Wilson that there is a common human desire for a particular type of place that beckons to the past. But I lack

Wilson's faith in the explanatory value of blind evolutionary processes. I don't think our nostalgia is the result of living in the sloped savanna near a water source that contributed to our survival. It is the ache of our hearts for a place where man and God once walked in peace, where human relationships were harmonious, and where death was not victorious.

Why God Won't Die

But we live in the real world now where this aching, this longing, can seem insatiable. There are plenty of ways in which we try to make the best of our three-score-plus-ten years on this pale-blue planet. Some seek meaning in relationships; others in the accumulation of stuff. But one thing is certain: we are all stuck here for some finite and indefinite period of time while we try to figure things out. And though the answers may be difficult to find, we are all highly motivated since we know our questions have an expiration date.

Perhaps this is why the religious impulse is so perennial. You have to wonder whether it is we who will not let go of it or the reverse, it refuses to let go of us. The religious outlook is where our collective human optimism and our longing for a place converge. It is the river flowing out of Eden. We walk along its banks and nourish ourselves with thoughts of home.

If the supernatural perspective is as delusional as some authors suggest it is, then it should be easy to shake off. But we seem infected by it with no sign of a remedy. And if evolution is so crafty as to hardwire, direct, supervise, plan, architect, et cetera, so much of our outlook, then why can it not rid us of this pernicious fantasy? Or might it be that the Darwinian metanarrative has met its match?

Jack Miles, professor of English and religious studies at the University of California at Irvine, touches on this theme is his article in *The Atlantic* titled "Why God Will Not Die."[9] He quotes Bertrand Russell (the same excerpt I quoted earlier in this chapter) as the basis of his own philosophy of life as a young man. Miles had copied the passage on a piece of paper and kept it in his wallet for a decade. But when his wallet was stolen and he went back to the original source to recopy the quote, he noticed a line that had initially escaped him.

The line that had first impressed Miles was this: "Only within the scaffolding of these truths, only on the firm foundation of unyielding despair, can the soul's habitation henceforth be safely built." The idea of unyielding despair as the foundation for constructing one's meaning was motivational for him. But a decade later, as Miles rewrote the passage, Russell's admission that his claims were "nearly certain" dislodged his confidence.

"I noticed that I had no independent knowledge of the scientific basis for his existential claims," Miles writes. In other words, he couldn't give a scientific explanation for his secular values. The footings of his secular worldview were shaken when he discovered Russell's admission of uncertainty.

In the article Miles gives a brief outline of the development of his perspective of science, philosophy, and religion throughout his life. He concludes that, like Russell, we can only be *nearly* certain of the truths that form the foundation for our lives. But he recognizes that despite our unavoidable and incurable ignorance, we still must build something.

> But when life refuses to wait any longer and the great game begins whether you have suited up or not, then a demand arises that religion—or some expedient no more fully rational than religion—must meet. You're going to go with something. Whatever it is, however rigorous it may claim to be as either science or religion, you're going to know that you have no perfect warrant for it. Yet, whatever you call it, you're going to go with it anyway, aren't you?[10]

Miles's central argument throughout the autobiographical narrative is that we should be more empathetic of our fellow creatures. We are all in the same boat, rowing through a deep mist and hoping to arrive safely at some desirable shore. But it is our desire to know, and our corporate need to build (to use Russell's metaphor), that compels us forward. "Humans seek closure," Miles writes, "which should make religious pluralists of us all."

But is this the best we can do? Can we do nothing more than say that the secular and the religious share a foundation of ignorance from which to construct meaning? Do our ideals really have to be disconnected from the real world? If the answer is yes, than the most basic of human values are by definition irrational.

Optimism and Reality

That is at the heart of the philosophy known as existentialism, which Miles references in one of the quotations above. Existentialism basically says that the universe is cold and indifferent and that we must choose to make our own meaning in the face of insignificance. There is no objective purpose for our lives. The basis of existential thought is that we must embrace values that have no rational explanation.

If the universe doesn't care, you should care anyway, the existentialist says. Just take a blind leap of faith and embrace your preferred value system. Miles acknowledges in his article "Why God Will Not Die" that even the secularist is forced to construct a value system to make life worth living; but it is a value system for which he cannot provide a rational foundation. If we assume naturalism, we must pull ourselves up by our bootstraps, turn a stiff face toward a cruel universe, and carve out a living for ourselves by constructing our own values as we go along.

Ultimately, all of our striving and hoping mean nothing. Sure, they are important to us personally, but in the grand scheme of things, the cosmos doesn't care. And our actions cannot change reality.

But what if there is more to reality than nature? What if behind nature there is a personal and powerful source? What if he cares? What if our values actually flow from him? What if our optimism is a by-product of his promise to one day make all things new?

In the end, only the gospel is powerful enough to reconcile human optimism with reality. The gospel offers an explanation for the world we live in, a remedy for the suffering we face, and the hope of a future place where all things will eventually work together for good and where our greatest foes—sin, death, and the grave—will be forever vanquished.

The follower of Christ does not defy the real world in order to construct such values. His or her values are an extension of the Christian view of reality, a rational response to the way things are and the way things will be. In Christianity, optimism is not irrational but is a logical response to a God who has conquered the curse of sin.

The charge that Christianity is irrational is increasingly losing sway in Thomas's mind. As the tables are turned, rather quickly and powerfully Zach's worldview appears incapable of providing a rational explanation of the world and human experience.

Conclusion

Hoax or Hope

I believe in Christianity as I believe that the
sun has risen—not only because I see it,
but because by it I see everything else.

C. S. Lewis, "Is Theology Poetry?"

I grew up in a blue-collar neighborhood of a small mid-
western town situated in the plains of central Illinois and
surrounded by cornfields as far as the eye can see. The town
of Alton, about an hour from our house, regularly made
national news for flooding. Alton sits in the middle of the
Illinois River basin, which makes it easy prey for rising
floodwaters.

My family would make annual trips to this area of the
state, typically in autumn when the river would be lined
with multicolored trees. As a kid I remember playing along

the riverbank and skipping rocks or throwing in sticks to watch them float away with the current. But when we would hike the trails up to a high lookout point in a nearby state park, we could see that what initially looked like one river where we were playing was actually three rivers: the Illinois, the Missouri, and the Mississippi.

Similarly, Thomas feels that his intellectual journey of looking at Christianity afresh, in response to his roommate's challenge, has given him a vantage point from which to see the many tributaries of the human experience converging into one powerful explanation. In Christianity, the streams of goodness and beauty, of right and wrong, and of religious impulse and human optimism all merge together in a formidable torrent.

That's because the gospel not only offers an explanation of the origins of the universe and the historical facts regarding the person of Jesus; it also sheds light on what it means to be human. We feel a certain way about moral categories, for example, because these things are real. We long to know God, and in the gospel we find that God has taken on flesh to make this possible. We hope for a better future and find that Jesus offers us even more.

Nothing is wasted in the gospel. There, all is redeemed and eventually set right by the one who created all things. History marches to the cadence of God's providence and for the purpose of his glory. Our lives blossom in this stream. It is the source of living water. But apart from the gospel, humanity withers and perishes.

If Thomas begins with the assumption that nature is all that exists, then what it means to be human is lost in a myriad of scientific nullifications. In atheism the things that make life worth living are considered illusions—perhaps helpful or meaningful illusions, but illusions nonetheless. And the best one can do is to fabricate significance and purpose for which there is not, and indeed cannot be, a rational foundation.

Eternal, impersonal, and mindless matter cannot establish a foundation for human flourishing. Can the personal come from the impersonal? Can the rational come from the irrational? No, it cannot. According to atheism, we are insignificant links in the long tiresome chain of causation binding humanity's hopes to natural explanations.

This is well illustrated in the moving story of Jennifer Fulwiler in her memoir *Something Other Than God*. She was raised in a completely secular household and did not become a Christian until adulthood. In a video interview about her story, she summarized the change in her thinking that ultimately culminated in her conversion:

> Before I got to the point that I could really start researching faith with an open mind, something had to happen. And for me that occurred after my first child was born. I looked down and thought "what is this baby" and I thought, *well from a pure atheist materialist perspective, he is a collection of randomly evolved chemical reactions.* And I realized, if that's true, then all the love I feel for him . . . it's all nothing more than

chemical reactions in our brains. And I looked down at him and realized that's not true. That's not the truth.[1]

Lying in her hospital bed, she was faced with the choice of dismissing her love for her child as a mere chemical reaction in her brain or exchanging her atheistic worldview for one big enough to account for the human experience.

A skeptic friend once asked me if I experience cognitive dissonance as a Christian. Cognitive dissonance is a psychological term for believing one thing to be true but experiencing the opposite. When we encounter new information that doesn't fit our current paradigm, we experience psychological conflict as we try to protect our old way of thinking.

My friend described how he felt that his journey from faith to atheism resulted in a complete loss of this kind of dissonance. In embracing secularism, he said he was able to leave behind beliefs that didn't line up with the real world. I can certainly empathize with some of his feelings that his fundamentalist past was out of step with reality.

But though he walked away from Christianity, he still treats things like love, personhood, free will, and morality as real entities worthy of his attention and pursuit. He now lives with a set of values that make sense only from the Christian point of view. He cannot offer a rational explanation for them since his worldview is traced back to irrational causes. If this doesn't cause cognitive dissonance, then I'm not sure what could.

The British author Dorothy Sayers once said, "It is fatal

to let people suppose that Christianity is only a mode of feeling; it is vitally necessary to insist that it is first and foremost a rational explanation of the universe."[2] The gospel offers a rational explanation because it begins with Mind and not mere matter. There's a rational source behind the created world: in the beginning was the Word.

But the gospel does better still. It not only offers a rational explanation of the universe; it offers a foundation for our optimism. In the gospel, optimism and reality are forever reconciled. As John said, "The law was given through Moses; grace and truth came through Jesus Christ" (John 1:17).

The Christian view is that God is an eternal and personal mind behind the created world. And it teaches that he actually visited his creation. So instead of our optimism being the most irrational thing about us, something we concoct for ourselves despite the facts, it is grounded in a promise that was validated in the historical events of the incarnation and the resurrection. The same Jesus whom the disciples saw after the crucifixion and burial, and whom they saw ascend into heaven, has promised to return and with his return to make all things new.

But we live in the mire of the in-between, where suffering and hope overlap. We've tasted and seen that the Lord is good, but this fallen world tends to leave a horrid aftertaste. It's not uncommon, nor is it wrong, for Thomas to entertain doubt. But as he works through his doubts, he still believes. James Smith paints a helpful picture of this landscape of doubt amid belief:

On the other hand, even as faith endures in our secular age, believing doesn't come easy. Faith is fraught; confession is haunted by an inescapable sense of its contestability. We don't believe instead of doubting; we believe while doubting. We're all Thomas now.

The wager of this book . . . is that most of us live in this cross-pressured space, where both our agnosticism and our devotion are mutually haunted and haunting. If our only guides were new atheists or religious fundamentalists, we would never know that this vast, contested terrain even existed, even though most of us live in this space every day.[3]

Thomas and Zach are committed to walking this terrain together, though their lives will follow different trajectories, and their friendship will take new form over the years. They've both adopted a specific story, an account of reality, for which neither can fully provide physical proof. And to a large extent, they share a common set of values, for which Thomas's worldview alone can provide a rational explanation.

For now, Zach is comfortable living in an atheistic world while borrowing values from his Christian past. He's happy to be rid of the baggage from his fundamentalist background, and he's hopeful for the future. He's betting that eternal, impersonal, and mindless matter will provide a better life and a brighter future.

But the final chapter of the atheist novel will not be so kind. Chance, who once played the hero, is revealed as humanity's archenemy. With a maniacal laugh he mocks us for ever thinking our ambitions and convictions meant anything at all. He scoffs at our misplaced confidence in evolution to lead us anywhere except into more illusions. And as the sun reaches the zenith of its fury, we read the last word on the last page. "Despair," we read aloud, as the Red Giant snuffs out what little life—if ever we should have called it that—remains on our little planet. The End.

The human experience is either the greatest hoax ever or it is a clue to the nature of reality. Either all our deepest hopes converge into one powerful explanation that only the gospel is vast enough to channel, or they dissipate like a mist under the rising sun. But if—in our striving and suffering, our loving and longing—we will just tune in, then we will hear nature's primitive call, the echo of Eden, bidding us to come and drink at the fountain of living water.

One story begins in chance and ends in chaos. Another begins with the Word and ends in life. Choose your story wisely.

Acknowledgments

The theologian Reinhold Niebuhr once quipped, "Nothing we do, however virtuous, can be accomplished alone."[1] He was right. That is certainly the case with this book. Perhaps I should first thank the publisher who was willing to make it possible. The team at Crossway has been great to work with. Dave DeWit (who still spells his name wrong) and the editing ninja Thom Notaro are gracious beyond measure.

I want to thank my wife, April, and my children, Isaiah, Micah, Josiah, and Addilynn Joy. You sacrificially support me by letting me steal away to coffee shops to punch at my keyboard and work on projects like this. You do so out of love for me and the hope that such undertakings will be used by God for something greater. You all are a greater treasure to me than anything I may ever get in print. If my life were a book, the dedication on every page would carry your names.

I also want to thank my mom, Nannette, who, among her countless contributions to my life, helped with the kids while I finished the rough draft of this book in the Upper Peninsula of Michigan. I'll not soon forget that snowy December day while I knocked out the final pages from the upper room at Donckers in downtown Marquette. Aunt Toni and Uncle Kevin, my cousins Nicole and Dave Mahaffey, and their children, Jillian, Cameron, Brianna, and Karlee, thank you guys for helping entertain the DeWitt crew and for the unforgettable Christmas at the lodge. And I have to give a Yooper shout out to Presbyterian Point for hosting our big Italian family festival.

I want to thank the Southern Baptist Theological Seminary and Boyce College for letting me teach classes on worldview and philosophy, and my annual winter course on C. S. Lewis. I also want to thank my students, who sharpen me more than they may realize. Their input and interaction on these topics have been an invaluable resource for refining this message.

I would like to thank my church, Highview Baptist Church, and all of the servant leaders there who have encouraged me over the years. The opportunities to serve in various capacities, not least of which is the Campus Church, have made an indelible mark on my approach to ministry. I hope you see this book as the overflow of your ministry.

I would like to thank Daniel and Molly Patz, and the Patz family in general, in honor of the legacy of Northland International University and Northland Ministries, for their gracious hospitality over the academic year 2014–2015. I penned many pages of this book while on that special and beautiful campus. More importantly, I formed friendships there that I pray will last a lifetime.

Finally, I want to give thanks to God the Father for his saving grace. If I did a cost-benefit analysis of the cross, I would have to conclude that it was a poor investment if it was about me. But, praise God, it was about a much higher aim: the nations, gathered by the Spirit, crowded around the throne of the Son, for the glory of the Father.

I'm thankful to be a recipient of God's blessed atonement. The only really good thing about me is the gospel. I'm so very thankful for it. Of this gospel I pray I'm never ashamed. And I pray the same for anyone reading these words.

Notes

Introduction: Reality Used to Be a Friend of Mine

1. C. S. Lewis, *God in the Dock: Essays on Theology and Ethics* (New York: HarperCollins, 2001), 101.

Chapter 1: Much Ado about Nothing

1. G. K. Chesterton, *The Everlasting Man* (New York: Dodd, Mead, 1944), xi.
2. Ibid., xiii.
3. Ibid., xii.
4. C. S. Lewis, *Surprised by Joy: The Shape of My Early Life* (New York: Harcourt, 1955), 213.
5. Larry Taunton, "Listening to Young Atheists: Lessons for a Stronger Christianity," *The Atlantic*, June 6, 2013, http://www.theatlantic.com/national/archive/2013/06/listening-to-young-atheists-lessons-for-a-stronger-christianity/276584.
6. Peter Boghossian, *A Manual for Creating Atheists* (Durham, NC: Pitchstone, 2013), 2.
7. Ibid.
8. Ibid.
9. Guy P. Harrison, *50 Simple Questions for Every Christian* (Amherst, NY: Prometheus, 2013), 13.
10. "How Did the Atom Obtain Its Name?," *Physics & Astronomy Online*, accessed January 10, 2014, http://www.physlink.com/Education/AskExperts/ae622.cfm.
11. "Lawrence Krauss on 'A Universe from Nothing,'" NPR, January 13, 2012, http://www.npr.org/2012/01/13/145175263/lawrence-krauss-on-a-universe-from-nothing.

12. Richard Dawkins, *River out of Eden: A Darwinian View of Life* (New York: Basic Books, 1995), 133. Cf. a lightly edited form of this quote in an essay adapted from chap. 4, "God's Utility Function," extracted in *Scientific American* (November 1995), http://www.physics.ucla.edu/~chester/CES/may98/dawkins.html.

13. See James Beilby, ed., *Naturalism Defeated: Essays on Alvin Plantinga's Evolutionary Argument against Naturalism* (Ithaca, NY: Cornell University Press, 2002).

14. Crispin Sartwell, "Irrational Atheism," *The Atlantic*, October 11, 2014, http://www.theatlantic.com/national/archive/2014/10/a-leap-of-atheist-faith/381353.

15. Alex Rosenberg, *The Atheist's Guide to Reality: Enjoying Life without Illusions* (New York: Norton, 2011), 18.

16. Julian Baggini, *Atheism: A Very Short Introduction* (New York: Oxford University Press, 2003), 6.

17. Julian Baggini, "Is There a Real You?" (lecture presented at TEDxYouth@Manchester, Miami, Florida, November 2011), http://www.ted.com/talks/julian_baggini_is_there_a_real_you.

18. H. G. Wells, *The Outline of History: Being a Plain History of Life and Mankind* (n.p.: Project Gutenberg, 2014), Kindle edition, introduction.

19. Cynthia Haven, "Lost in the Shadow of C. S. Lewis' Fame / Joy Davidman Was a Noted Poet, a Feisty Communist and a Free Spirit," SFGate, January 1, 2006, http://www.sfgate.com/books/article/ESSAY-Lost-in-the-shadow-of-C-S-Lewis-fame-2524646.php.

20. Lyle W. Dorsett, "Helen Joy Davidman (Mrs. C. S. Lewis) 1915–1960: A Portrait," *C. S. Lewis Institute*, accessed December 17, 2014, http://www.cslewisinstitute.org/node/31.

Chapter 2: The Cosmic Song

1. Stan and Jan Berenstain, *The Berenstain Bears' Big Book of Science and Nature* (New York: Random House, 1997), 11.

2. Robert Jastrow, *God and the Astronomers* (New York: Norton, 1978), 16.

3. Ibid., 25.

4. Ibid., 26.

5. A. D. Chernin, V. Ya. Frenkel, and E. A. Tropp, *Alexander Fried-mann: The Man Who Made the Universe Expand* (New York: Cambridge University Press, 1993), 175.

6. Richard Dawkins, *The Magic of Reality: How We Know What's Really True* (New York: Free Press, 2011), 96.

7. Arno Penzias, interview by Malcolm Browne, "Clues to the Universe's Origin Expected," *New York Times*, March 12, 1978.

Chapter 3: The Major Anthem

1. Quoted in William Federer, *George Washington Carver: His Life and Faith in His Own Words* (St. Louis, MO: Amerisearch, 2002), 71–73.

2. Gerard Manley Hopkins, *Poems* (London: Humphrey Milford, 1918), accessed April 2, 2014, http://www.bartleby.com/122/7.html.

3. Timothy Keller, *The Reason for God: Belief in an Age of Skepticism* (New York: Dutton, 2008), xii–xiii.

4. Christopher Hitchens and Douglas Wilson, *Is Christianity Good for the World? A Debate* (Moscow, ID: Canon, 2008), 58.

5. John Lennox, *God's Undertaker: Has Science Buried God?* (Oxford, England: Lion Hudson, 2009), Kindle edition, chap. 2.

6. C. S. Lewis, *The Magician's Nephew*, in *The Chronicles of Narnia* (New York: Collier, 1970), 101–2, 116.

7. Laura Miller, *The Magician's Book: A Skeptic's Adventures in Narnia* (New York: Little, Brown, 2008), 3.

8. Ibid., 25.

Chapter 4: The Minor Key

1. http://www.ispot.tv/ad/7noF/allstate-good-life.

2. Kai Nielson, "Why Should I Be Moral?," *American Philosophical Quarterly* 21 (1984): 90.

3. Daniel Burke, "Satanists Unveil Design for OK Statehouse Statue," *CNN*, January 7, 2014, http://religion.blogs.cnn.com/2014/01/07/satanists-unveil-design-for-statehouse-statue.

4. Richard Dawkins, *River out of Eden: A Darwinian View of Life* (New York: Basic Books, 1995), 133.

5. Alex Rosenberg, *The Atheist's Guide to Reality: Enjoying Life without Illusions* (New York: Norton, 2011), ix.

6. Steve Turner, "Creed," quoted in *Verita Lux Mea*, August 11, 2007, http://veritasluxmea-freshmao.blogspot.com/2007/08/poems-creed-and-chance.html.

7. An outstanding article that gives a concise biography of C. E. M. Joad, focusing on his conversion to Christianity, is Joel D. Heck, "From Vocal Agnostic to Reluctant Convert: The Influence of C. S. Lewis on the Conversion C. E. M. Joad," http://www.joelheck.com/resources/CEM%20Joad,%20Intersections%20with%20CS%20Lewis%20for%20Sehnsucht.pdf.

8. C. E. M. Joad, *The Recovery of Belief: A Restatement of Christian Philosophy* (London: Faber and Faber, 1951), 23.

9. Ibid., 13.

10. Ibid., 79.

11. Ibid., 81.

12. Ibid., 82.

13. C. S. Lewis, *Mere Christianity* (New York: Macmillan, 1952), 120.

Chapter 5: Haunted by Transcendence

1. James K. A. Smith, *How (Not) to Be Secular* (Grand Rapids, MI: Eerdmans, 2014), 1.

2. "The Global Religious Landscape," *Religion & Public Life*, Pew Research Center, December 18, 2012, http://www.pewforum.org/2012/12/18/global-religious-landscape-exec.

3. Heather Horn, "Where Does Religion Come From?," *The Atlantic*, August 17, 2011, http://www.theatlantic.com/entertainment/archive/2011/08/where-does-religion-come-from/243723.

4. Colin Duriez, *The C. S. Lewis Encyclopedia: A Complete Guide to His Life, Thought, and Writings* (Wheaton, IL: Crossway, 2000), 175.

5. Arthur James Balfour, *Theism and Humanism* (London: Hodder and Stoughton, 1915), 136.

6. Dinesh D'Souza, "Conversion of a Cynic," *Crisis*, August 1, 1984, http://www.crisismagazine.com/1984/conversion-of-a-cynic.

7. Malcolm Muggeridge, *Chronicles of a Wasted Life* (New York: Morrow, 1973), 124–25.

8. Malcolm Muggeridge, "Christ and the Media," *Journal of the Evangelical Theological Society* 21, no 3 (1978): 193, http://www.etsjets.org/files/JETS-PDFs/21/21-3/21-3-pp193–198_JETS.pdf.

9. Ibid., 197–98.

10. C. S. Lewis, *Miracles: A Preliminary Study* (New York: Macmillan, 1947), 21.

Chapter 6: What If God Were One of Us?

1. Nelson Glueck, *Rivers in the Desert* (New York: Farrar, Straus, and Cudahy, 1959), 136.

2. "King Solomon's Copper Mines?," *Science Daily*, October 28, 2008, www.sciencedaily.com/releases/2008/10/081027174545.htm.

3. Joe Carter, "Snickering at FoxNews While Getting Duped by 'Zealot' Author," *Patheos*, July 29, 2013, http://www.patheos.com/blogs/getreligion/2013/07/snickering-at-foxnews-while-getting-duped-by-zealot-author/#ixzz3L2x1g7Hb.

4. Ibid.

5. Dale Martin, "Still a Firebrand, 2,000 Years Later," *New York Times*, August 5, 2013, http://www.nytimes.com/2013/08/06/books/reza-aslans-zealot-the-life-and-times-of-jesus-of-nazareth.html?pagewanted=all&_r=0.

6. Greg Carey, "Reza Aslan on Jesus: A Biblical Scholar Responds," *Huffington Post*, July 30, 2013, http://www.huffingtonpost.com/greg-carey/reza-aslan-on-jesus_b_3679466.html.

7. Craig Evans, "Reza Aslan Tells an Old Story about Jesus," *Christianity Today*, August 9, 2013, http://www.christianitytoday.com/ct/2013/august-web-only/zealot-reza-aslan-tells-same-old-story-about-jesus.html?start=3.

8. Reza Aslan, *Zealot: The Life and Times of Jesus of Nazareth* (New York: Random House, 2013), 13.

9. W. Ward Gasque, *Sir William M. Ramsay: Archaeologist and New Testament Scholar: A Survey of His Contribution to the Study of the New Testament* (Grand Rapids, MI: Baker, 1967), 17, accessed November 25, 2014, http://www.biblicalstudies.org.uk/pdf/ramsay/ramsay_gasque.pdf.

10. Sir William Mitchell Ramsay, *The Bearing of Recent Discovery on the Trustworthiness of the New Testament*, 2nd ed. (London: Hodder and Stoughton, 1915), 38.

11. Ibid., 85.

12. Sir William M. Ramsay, *St. Paul the Traveller and the Roman Citizen*, 14, quoted in Gasque, *Sir William M. Ramsay*, 28.

13. C. S. Lewis, "The Shocking Alternative," chap. 3 in *Mere Christianity* (New York: Macmillan, 1952).

14. J. Warner Wallace, *Cold-Case Christianity: A Homicide Detective Investigates the Claims of the Gospels* (Colorado Springs, CO: David C. Cook, 2013), 28.

15. Gary R. Habermas and Michael R. Licona, *The Case for the Resurrection of Jesus* (Grand Rapids, MI: Kregel, 2004), 44.

16. Ibid., 48–75.

17. Wallace, *Cold-Case Christianity*, 50.

Chapter 7: Our Stubborn Smile

1. Tali Sharot, "The Optimism Bias," *Time*, May 28, 2011, http://content.time.com/time/health/article/0,8599,2074067-1,00.html.

2. Bertrand Russell, *The Basic Writings of Bertrand Russell* (New York: Routledge, 2009), 39.

3. Douglas Hyde, "Superheroes Rise in Tough Times," CNN, March 20, 2009, http://www.cnn.com/2009/SHOWBIZ/books/03/18/superhero.history/index.html?iref=24hours.

4. "History of 'In God We Trust,'" U.S. Department of the Treasury, accessed January 23, 2014, http://www.treasury.gov/about/education/Pages/in-god-we-trust.aspx.

5. David Greenberg, "The Pledge of Allegiance: Why We're Not One Nation 'Under God,'" *Slate*, June 28, 2002, http://www.slate.com/articles/news_and_politics/history_lesson/2002/06/the_pledge_of_allegiance.html.

6. Edward O. Wilson, *The Meaning of Human Existence* (New York: Liveright, 2014), 144.

7. J. R. R. Tolkien, *The Letters of J. R. R. Tolkien* (New York: Houghton Mifflin Harcourt, 2014), Kindle edition, to Christopher Tolkien, January 30, 1945.

8. Jo Piazza, "Audiences Experience 'Avatar' Blues," CNN, January 11, 2010, http://www.cnn.com/2010/SHOWBIZ/Movies/01/11/avatar.movie.blues.

9. Jack Miles, "Why God Will Not Die," *The Atlantic*, November 17, 2014, http://www.theatlantic.com/magazine/archive/2014/12/why-god-will-not-die/382231/?single_page=true.

10. Ibid.

Conclusion: Hoax or Hope

1. Jennifer Fulwiler, "Jennifer Fulwiler's Journey from Atheism to Christ," accessed September 22, 2014, https://www.youtube.com/watch?v=RETMFkoZEP0.

2. Dorothy Sayers, *Creed or Chaos?* (New York: Harcourt, Brace, 1949), 28.

3. James K. A. Smith, *How (Not) to Be Secular* (Grand Rapids, MI: Eerdmans, 2014), 4.

Acknowledgments

1. Reinhold Niebuhr, *The Irony of American History* (Chicago: University of Chicago Press, 2008), 63.

Index

It's time to make a choice.

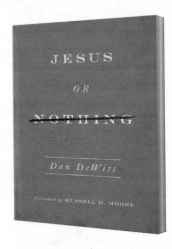

Many young adults are abandoning the Christian faith, convinced that it's an outdated and uneducated belief system. In *Jesus or Nothing*, Dan DeWitt describes the rock-solid foundation for life that Christians enjoy in and through the gospel—offering an explanation for our existence, grace for our guilt, and meaning for our mortality.

"DeWitt clearly demonstrates that there are really only two worldviews in constant conflict: theism versus nihilism. Any thinking person will benefit from reading this important book."

R. ALBERT MOHLER JR., President and Joseph Emerson Brown Professor of Christian Theology, The Southern Baptist Theological Seminary

"Atheism is often portrayed as the only intelligent worldview, but this book dispels the fog of that myth. I heartily recommend Jesus or Nothing *to anyone struggling to sort through the shrill, confusing voices trying to tell us what matters most."*

TED CABAL, General Editor, *The Apologetics Study Bible*